Musicians of Mars II

Foreword

"There is still a tendency in each separate unit ... to be a one-handed puncher. By that I mean the rifleman wants to shoot, the tanker to charge, the artilleryman to fire. ... That is not the way to win battles. If the band played a piece first with the piccolo, then with the brass horn, then with the clarinet, and then with the trumpet, there would be a hell of a lot of noise but no music. To get harmony in music, each instrument must support the others. To get harmony in battle, each weapon must support the other. Team play wins. You musicians of Mars ... must come into the concert at the proper place and at the proper time."

MG George S. Patton Jr.
Address to the 2nd Armored Division
Fort Benning, GA, 08 JUL 1941

In TRADOC Pamphlet 525-3-1, The U.S. Army Operating Concept [AOC]: Win in a Complex World, 2020-2040, the 38th Chief of Staff of the Army, GEN Raymond T. Odierno, states: "The AOC's vision of future armed conflict considers both continuities in war's nature and changes in its character. Conflicts in the future, like those in the past, will ultimately be resolved on land. Hence the concept recognizes that Army forces will be essential components of joint operations to create sustainable political outcomes while defeating enemies and adversaries who will challenge U.S. advantages in all domains: land, air, maritime, space, and cyberspace."

The AOC states: "One of our most important duties as Army professionals is to think clearly about the problem of future armed conflict. ... The environment the Army will operate in is unknown. The enemy is unknown, the location is unknown, and the coalitions involved are unknown. The problem we are focusing on is how to 'Win in a Complex World.' "

Units and leaders must train with the mindset of massing and synchronizing efforts, from direct-fire weapons systems to electronic warfare to information operations, throughout the range of potential decisive action environments. Commanders must develop training plans that account for enablers that are not organic to their units, but likely to be attached during operations. Leaders must plan and execute actions at critical times and places on the battlefield to achieve intended outcomes. Successful leaders will account for the vast array of hybrid threat and friendly capabilities, allowing them to use the appropriate tools and enablers at the appropriate times on the battlefield, synchronized with the range of available combat power.

Similar to the conductor of an orchestra, combat leaders must synchronize all of the "instruments" available to produce a "symphony" of effort on the battlefield, rather than the noise of individual instruments not in harmony with others. Playing the correct notes at the correct times is essential to achieving maximum effectiveness, seizing and maintaining initiative, and decisively defeating the hybrid threat. GEN Patton's "harmony" of 1941 is "synchronization" of today's unified land operations and decisive action.

Musicians of Mars II is an update from the original 1990 publication, accounting for changes in today's environment and doctrine. It tells a story of synchronization from the maneuver team commander's perspective. There are no perfect solutions, but the intent is to get leaders to think throughout the range of possibilities and capabilities, coordinating assets and efforts throughout the battlefield to achieve victory. Although the story and characters are fictional, the successes and failures portrayed are applicable to units currently training and operating worldwide. The goal is for the reader to better understand synchronization and how to better prepare themselves, their units, and their Soldiers to become "Musicians of Mars." And in doing so, we "Win in a Complex World."

Willard M. Burleson III
BG, USA
Director, Mission Command Center of Excellence

Musicians of Mars II

Table of Contents

Center For Army Lessons Learned

Director	COL Paul P. Reese
CALL Analyst	Nathan B. Blood

This handbook is a sequel to CALL Publication 90-6, *The Musicians of Mars: A Story of Synchronization for the Company/Team Commander*, June 1990.

The Secretary of the Army has determined that the publication of this periodical is necessary in the transaction of the public business as required by law of the Department.

Unless otherwise stated, whenever the masculine or feminine gender is used, both are intended.

Note: Any publications (other than CALL publications) referenced in this product, such as ARs, ADPs, ADRPs, ATPs, FMs, and TMs, must be obtained through your pinpoint distribution system.

Introduction

The nations of Bolcavia and Arcania, including any references to cities, towns, or other locations, are fictional, as are the characters of this story. Any references to actual names or places are coincidental and not intended. References to U.S. and coalition forces and previous combat operations are provided only for context in the fictional scenario.

This short story was written to emphasize critical synchronization tasks, combat leadership principles, and factors for consideration, primarily for company/team commanders but also for leaders throughout tactical-level units. The importance of integrating and synchronizing available combat power, both lethal and nonlethal, in the decisive action environment against potential hybrid threats is critical to unit success on the battlefield.

This project is an update to *The Musicians of Mars*, June 1990, a publication originally developed by the Center for Army Lessons Learned (CALL). This update accounts for changes to doctrine, training, and technology as applicable in today's decisive action environment and contemporary worldwide hybrid threats.

When this project started, CALL identified specific tasks from Army Doctrine Reference Publication (ADRP) 1-03, *The Army Universal Task List*, October 2015, that apply to offense, defense, and stability operations in combined arms maneuver (CAM), wide area security (WAS), and stability operations. These tasks were coordinated with the Maneuver Center of Excellence and the National Training Center to emphasize specific areas of importance. Current doctrinal references were applied in the context of the story. Many of these references are listed below. In addition to those listed, principles and tactics, techniques, and procedures from Army techniques publications, training circulars, and field manuals applicable to all warfighting functions were used in development. The specific tasks applied to the scenario are:

1. Conduct Tactical Maneuver, Army Tactical Task (ART) 1.2

2. Conduct Passage of Lines, ART 1.2.8

3. Occupy an Attack and Assault Position, ART 1.5.2

4. Occupy and Establish a Battle or Defensive Position, ART 1.5.3

5. Overcome Barriers, Obstacles, and Mines, ART 1.6.1

6. Conduct Breaching Operations, ART 1.6.1.1

7. Conduct Gap-Crossing Operations, ART 1.6.1.3

8. Enhance Movement and Maneuver, ART 1.6.2

9. Conduct Countermobility Operations, ART 1.7

10. Conduct Reconnaissance, ART 1.8

11. Conduct Maneuver Support Operations, ART 1.10

12. Integrate Fires, ART 3.1

13. Employ Fires, ART 3.2.1

14. Conduct Surface to Surface Attack, ART 3.2.1.1

15. Employ Close Air Support, ART 3.2.1.2.2

16. Employ Air and Missile Defense, ART 3.4

17. Provide Combat Casualty Care, ART 4.3.1

18. Provide Medical Evacuation (Air and Ground), ART 4.3.2

19. Prepare for Tactical Operations, ART 5.1.2

20. Reorganize Units as Part of a Reconstitution Effort, ART 5.1.3.6.1

21. Conduct Public Affairs Operations, ART 5.7

22. Conduct Electronic Warfare, ART 5.9.2

23. Synchronize Information-Related Capabilities, ART 5.12

24. Conduct Civil Affairs Operations, ART 5.15

25. Prepare Fighting Positions, ART 6.6.1.2

26. Prepare Protective Positions, ART 6.6.1.3

27. Implement Operations Security, ART 6.10

28. Assault an Objective, ART 7.1.2.2

29. Conduct a Counterattack, ART 7.1.2.3

30. Conduct an Area Defense, ART 7.2.2

31. Attack by Fire an Enemy Force or Position, ART 7.5.1

Through the mission command philosophy, commanders understand that subordinates and staffs require a clear intent to guide their actions. Leaders must be able to clearly portray intent to subordinate leaders, enable and empower subordinate leaders to execute critical tasks, and continue to lead and assess throughout execution of missions to ensure success at all levels.

Training at individual and collective levels sets the conditions for synchronization. Standards must be met or set. Leaders must integrate key assets and enablers into collective unit training plans. In many cases, this requires creativity and initiative to account for those assets that may not be organic to the training unit. Leaders must identify the critical mission tasks across the spectrum of CAM/WAS, actively pursue available resources for training, and execute training to the established standards. Each piece of the orchestra must practice individually, then collectively, in order to achieve the harmony of synchronization.

Team Badger
Battle Position Badger
H+6 Hours (1200L)

The lingering sulfur odor of gunpowder, mixed in the haze of the dust and smoke of battle, dominated the senses of CPT Fred Morris, commander of Team Badger. He sat amid the wreckage of what used to be some of the world's finest combat machines, M1A2 Abrams tanks and M2A3 Bradley fighting vehicles. Now most of his company's tanks and Brads were mere smoking hulks, emanating the distinct smell of burning electronics to add another element to the senses of the dismal scene before him.

He sat, quietly reflecting on the sequence of events that led to the destruction of his beloved team. His mind raced as he recounted how the enemy force, so much more formidable than he had expected, employed assets, capabilities, and tactics that he had not taken into account. At the same time, he wondered why he was unable to bring to bear his own extensive combat power to earn decisive victory. He had felt so ready, so confident, and believed that his team had prepared so diligently. Yet, still they had been defeated so soundly. How could that be?

LTC Joe Milner, the task force commander, had given Team Badger the task to defend the center of the task force main battle area (MBA) in an area defense to destroy the attacking enemy motorized rifle brigade. Specifically, CPT Morris and Team Badger were to defend against the enemy's main effort motorized rifle battalion in Battle Position (BP) Badger, along the enemy's most likely avenue of approach. That motorized rifle battalion plowed through Team Badger as if it were not even there.

CPT Morris felt anger and frustration at the events he had not anticipated. How did his battle position get attacked by an apparent terrorist? Why did 200 refugees cross through the engagement area (EA) just minutes before the enemy attack forces arrived? These events created turmoil at critical times, affecting his team's ability to focus on the enemy's conventional formations. The presence of civilians caused hesitation and confusion over how to avoid killing them instead of the enemy. Or, was the enemy integrated, hiding among those supposed refugees? Did the enemy use the refugees as a means to gather intelligence prior to the attack? How could that be determined?

Fortunately, Team Dagger, the task force reserve under the command of CPT Gerald Crafton, had delivered a decisive blow to the enemy during a counterattack just before Team Badger's position was overrun. CPT Morris could not help but wonder if he would even be around to ponder his fate had Team Dagger not arrived and brought decisive firepower on the enemy main attack elements.

3

CPT Morris reflected on the words of the division commander, MG Tom Bolten, during the deployment ceremony at home station. MG Bolten reflected on his combat experiences 25 years earlier as a young company commander. The words echoed resonantly now as CPT Morris recalled the points about bringing all combat power to bear on the enemy at the appropriate times and places. He recalled the message about implementing mission command, understanding the commander's intent, and executing within that intent.

CPT Morris remembered thinking that technology and systems were well beyond those of 25 years ago, and doubting that MG Bolten's experiences were relevant on today's battlefield. Besides, CPT Morris' team consisted of noncommissioned officers with multiple years of combat experience in Afghanistan and Iraq, not the types of Soldiers with little or no combat experience who filled the ranks during MG Bolten's company command.

Ironically, CPT Crafton's father, Jack Crafton, had been a company commander with MG Bolten. But Crafton's company had been decimated by the enemy and MG Bolten's team saved the day with a decisive counterattack. The battle had been a case study at the Maneuver Captains Career Course (MCCC). Suddenly the depth of the irony hit CPT Morris. He now stood in CPT Jack Crafton's shoes, reflecting on what had gone so wrong in the throes of battle. How, then, could CPT Gerald Crafton have been so successful and decisive in his team's mission after the apparent failure of Team Badger?

CPT Morris wished he had more time to train and synchronize defense collective tasks at company level during home station training, but he had to prioritize training, and there just was not enough time to train every task. He recalled learning similar lessons at the National Training Center (NTC), but this mission was his first time conducting a live company defense. He thought, "If I had brought my doctrinal reference checklists for the defense and engagement area development, would I have been more successful in assigning priorities of work to my platoons?" He also recalled his instructors at the MCCC stressing the steps of EA development, and realized he had missed the opportunity to identify likely avenues of approach and determine the enemy scheme of maneuver. He knew he would have been more successful if he had rehearsed the EA and emplaced elements to observe dead space.

Although the battalion S-2 did a good job of providing the most likely enemy course of action, CPT Morris knew he should have refined the plan with reconnaissance at his level before completing the plan and issuing the company operation order (OPORD). He recalled how little time he had after he received the OPORD from the task force until he issued his warning order (WARNORD). When he issued the WARNORD, he should have issued priorities of work. But he had not. He knew he was defending, and he knew where. Now he thought to himself: "I could have better used other leaders in headquarters to assist with troop-leading procedures. Following reconnaissance, the company intelligence support team could have helped to refine the information received from the task force OPORD, and also helped me with Paragraph 1. The first sergeant and executive officer could have aided with Paragraph 4. The master gunner could have ensured vehicles were bore-sighted and provided more assistance on the tactical capabilities of the Bradley fighting vehicle." CPT Morris had failed to delegate responsibility for some of these key tasks, instead taking it upon himself. Additionally, he had taken for granted and assumed that many of these tasks would be accomplished. It was a blatant oversight.

A medic from Team Cobra jolted CPT Morris out of his thoughts and back to reality. "Sir, are you OK?"

At that point, CPT Morris realized that his team was not even able to treat and evacuate its own wounded Soldiers. He recalled instructing his own medic, SPC Atterbury, to establish a team casualty collection point (CCP) prior to the mission. Now he could not recall where the CCP was located. Did anyone else in the team know? If he did not know, how could they? Then, when both the medic and first sergeant, on whom Morris relied for his casualty evacuation (CASEVAC) plan, were killed in an early enemy artillery attack, the execution of any casualty treatment or evacuation plans was over. Suddenly he wondered how many combat lifesavers he had on the team. Who were they? If he did not know, who did? Why hadn't he thought of a backup plan for casualty treatment and evacuation in the event he lost his medic and first sergeant, as he did? Again, he reflected on the development of his plan. He should have had the first sergeant more involved to conduct CASEVAC rehearsals and include a CASEVAC section in Paragraph 4 of the OPORD. He should have had graphics that included CCPs and routes for his subordinate leaders. If the company had rehearsed the CASEVAC plan, the platoon sergeants could have assumed the responsibility when the first sergeant was killed.

"I'll be OK," Morris replied to the Team Cobra medic. "Please help out my other Soldiers. They need you more right now."

The medic left him with a bottle of water, for which CPT Morris was grateful. He was parched and near exhaustion as his mind continued to wander over the fateful course of events. What else had he missed?

CPT Morris began to recount the unfortunate sequence of events upon contact. Initial contact with the enemy forces came almost immediately after the detonation of an improvised explosive device (IED) on the right flank of the battle position, destroying one of the Brads and eliminating the crew from the fight before it really even began. It dawned on him that his team had not had a plan to maintain security of their fighting positions before occupying them. It was apparently too easy for the enemy to emplace an IED there. All the preparation of what seemed like an ideal battle position was lost because Team Badger had failed to maintain local security.

The distraction with the refugees almost immediately followed, causing confusion throughout the team on how to deal with civilians in the engagement area, knowing the enemy was closing rapidly. Between the IED incident and the refugees, CPT Morris considered his employment of his dismounted infantry squads. In reflection, they were focused solely on destruction of the enemy in the engagement area. CPT Morris had not given them a clear task and purpose to maintain security of the battle position and the engagement area, let alone position them to accomplish such a task.

> **POINT: Consider implied tasks, particularly security, while preparing a battle position and developing an engagement area.**

Although the task force had an evacuation plan, Team Badger was unable to communicate effectively with the native-speaking refugees. If only the Soldiers had been better prepared to deal with civilians on the battlefield. This certainly led to hesitation by the team as the enemy entered the engagement area. The team was ineffective in massing fires on the attacking formation. Were these events coordinated? And, as if "Murphy" himself were standing in the BP, that was the moment when radio communication became almost impossible. With only intermittent communication over the FM nets, CPT Morris was unable to direct his platoons and effectively engage the closing enemy forces. But they knew what to do, right? The OPORD brief to his platoon leaders (PLs) clearly laid out the plan. Shouldn't the tank and Bradley crews have known what to do?

> **POINT: Crews must understand and rehearse battle drills as outlined in Training Circular (TC) 3-21.8, *Infantry Rifle and Mechanized Platoon Collective Task Publication*, and TC 3-20.15, *Tank Platoon Collective Task Publication*. Leaders must ensure that crews are trained to standard on battle drills.**

> **POINT: With the modern hybrid threat, it is important to consider the range of potential enemy combatants and noncombatants that units may encounter on the battlefield. In synchronizing efforts, commanders must account for the range of possibilities. A hybrid threat is the "diverse and dynamic combination of regular forces, irregular forces, terrorist forces, and/or criminal elements unified to achieve mutually benefitting effects." (Army Doctrine Reference Publication 3-0, *Unified Land Operations*)**

The enemy battalion was able to reach the initial obstacles relatively unimpeded and begin breaching operations relatively unhindered when the team was finally able to coordinate some sort of direct fire on the enemy. But no sooner had the team begun to make a semblance of an organized defense than enemy artillery fires rained on the BP, taking a further toll on CPT Morris' combat power and again disrupting communication and execution of the fight in the engagement area. The artillery came in precise volleys, inflicting catastrophic damage to two of his platoons. It was as if the enemy had the 10-digit grid locations for each of his tanks and Bradleys. Did it? How could the enemy have been so accurate in targeting the BP?

He recalled a quote from his observer-coach/trainer (OC/T) during the last after action review at the NTC. "Security operations prevent enemy intelligence, surveillance, and reconnaissance assets from determining friendly locations, strengths, and weaknesses." Now he pondered, "Did I plan for emplacement of observation on all likely enemy avenues of approach? Come to think of it, we never really made sure that the area was clear of enemy personnel when we initially occupied. Enemy observation posts could be in the adjacent high terrain right now observing and reporting our activities. In the company we have nine rifle squads with 81 dismounted Soldiers who could have conducted patrols on the adjacent terrain, provided additional reconnaissance to me and the CoIST, and been better integrated in the direct-fire plan."

CPT Morris sheepishly pulled the crumpled decision support matrix (DSM) from his pocket. LTC Milner had specifically told the commanders to make sure they understood the critical events on the battlefield. CPT Morris looked at the star in his engagement area, indicating a potential breach of the obstacles by the enemy. It was one of the critical events. Yet he had not adequately developed the plan to support the commander's decision.

Suddenly he recalled the remote-controlled toy quadcopter that he had seen on several occasions during preparation of the BP. He had seen these in Voloslav on several occasions. They had become a trendy rage with the locals, especially the teenage kids. It made sense. They were quite popular back home, too. He had not thought much of it until now. But, why had the quadcopter been here, well outside the city? It seemed odd. Could it have provided enemy surveillance of his BP preparation? CPT Morris had not considered the possibility that the enemy might use the same unmanned aircraft system (UAS) reconnaissance techniques as U.S. forces. Now it dawned on him. That quadcopter had been hovering near the BP just moments before the destructive artillery attack began. With all of the chaos on the battlefield, CPT Morris had not given it a second thought. And now he realized that it was probably confirming locations that were discovered in the days before. He thought, "I should have checked with the task force tactical operations center. They probably would have been able to tell me if there were any friendly UAS in the area or if there was a threat of enemy UAS. As a matter of fact, I think I heard the S-2 mention something about them in an update."

The enemy artillery had been relentless, destroying several vehicles and causing numerous casualties. It seemed to last for hours. CPT Morris now remembered a similar artillery attack simulated on his team at the NTC. Fortunately the task force fire support officer (FSO) had allocated a Q36 radar critical friendly zone (CFZ) on his battle position, deemed critical to the task force defense. The artillery battalion had responded with a counterfire mission almost immediately as the radar acquired the enemy artillery. This brought an abrupt end to the enemy artillery attack, as the firing unit was destroyed by the counterfire mission. Now CPT Morris wondered why he had not thought to request a CFZ on his battle position. Wasn't this position just as critical in the defense? Perhaps a counterfire mission would have lessened the destructive power of the enemy artillery attack.

Nearly simultaneously with the artillery attack, an enemy attack helicopter engaged and destroyed two of the tanks in the center platoon of the defense. An Avenger team, a brigade asset attached to Team Badger, was killed during the initial artillery volleys before it could help protect against the attack aviation. It was the equivalent of a boxing match in which the opponent was throwing jabs, hooks, and haymakers, all sequentially timed and coordinated, leading to the inevitable knockout blow.

Why had Team Badger been unable to counter the enemy's coordinated and effective attack? CPT Morris glanced at the Avenger position. Although SGT Sandoval, the Avenger team chief, had recommended moving 200 meters to be better able to counter air threats, CPT Morris decided to have him remain in the BP, where he felt he could still counter air threats but also provide one more acquisition system with the Avenger Forward Looking Infrared (FLIR) system to supplement his defense in the battle position. As a result, the Avenger fell victim to the artillery barrage on the main battle position and was out of the fight. Now that CPT Morris thought about it more, asking SGT Sandoval to try to account for both air and ground threats probably distracted him from his primary mission of defending against air attacks.

> **POINT:** Systems and vehicles should be positioned to perform their primary missions and tasks. Avoid the temptation of planning the use of direct-fire systems that are secondary in nature. This may preclude performance of the primary mission of the vehicle or team.

CPT Morris returned to his analysis of the fight in the engagement area. Once Team Badger was able to orient fires on the enemy, it still was unable to make any serious impact on the approaching combat vehicles, even while they were momentarily stationary at the initial obstacles that shaped the engagement area. In fact, Team Badger's direct fires failed to achieve significant effects throughout the battle. Why had they been so ineffective? CPT Morris knew his crews were trained and competent in the crew drills. During training, his crews scored among the highest in the battalion during gunnery tables. Now he wondered if his home station collective training had been adequate for his platoons to achieve mastery on offensive and defensive tasks as a unit. Clearly they had been successful as individual crews, but did that ensure success collectively? Apparently not. Again, he reflected on the tools from MCCC. Perhaps leader training, followed by use and implementation in his platoon and company training exercises, could have provided better clarity and understanding to platoons and the entire company/team in performing the collective tasks necessary for a successful defensive operation.

Suddenly a sickening feeling washed over him. Thinking back to the BP preparation, he recalled adjusting the positions of his combat vehicles to take advantage of the reverse slope of a small ridge in the BP. Now he hesitantly pulled the map from his cargo pocket, the same map he had used for planning his BP and engagement area. He already knew what he would see.

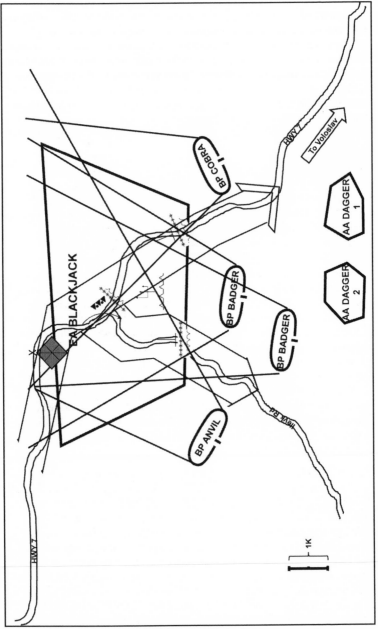

Figure 1-1. The Task Force Mustang engagement area.

CPT Morris recalled hastily giving the engineer platoon leader some guidance on establishing the obstacles in the engagement area. He had made some tweaks to locations and orientation of the planned obstacles, but for the most part he instructed the PL to emplace them in accordance with the plan published in the task force order. He thought, after having a chance to see the terrain, that his adjustments better shaped the engagement area. But again, he had not taken advantage of his own reconnaissance assets and refined the plan based on intelligence that could have been gathered in a thorough recon of the EA.

But then he had moved his positions. Now, as he stared down at his dog-eared map, he could see where he had marked the positions of the obstacles and each of his positions. The sickening feeling further developed as he mentally traced the maximum effective ranges of his weapons systems. After the change in locations, the obstacles designed to turn the enemy into the engagement area were a good 500 meters beyond even his longest-range weapons. [See Figure 1-1, preceding page.] And if the systems with the longest ranges were not within range, what about the systems with significantly shorter ranges? He had not even considered the range of his Javelins. He had placed them in, what he thought at the time, were great positions of cover and concealment. Now he realized they were not anywhere near where they could possibly engage the enemy effectively. "I knew where I wanted to kill the enemy, but my positioning did not allow us to mass fires at the decisive point in the EA." He remembered the master gunner and his duties and responsibilities. The master gunner is his team's expert in vehicle gunnery. He should be involved in any gunnery issues. He assists the commander in preparations for combat to ensure that every crew and platoon can make effective, lethal use of its firepower assets. SFC Schnell, his master gunner, had reminded him on several occasions that he was the technical expert who could assist the commander. He also was a fantastic NCO. Now CPT Morris thought, "I should have taken advantage of his expertise in developing the EA."

But hadn't his NCOs noticed this as they prepared their range cards? Did they prepare the range cards at all? CPT Morris was disgusted with himself as he realized he did not even know. He had not checked any range cards, nor had he assigned the responsibility to anybody else. He assumed that those things happened per standing operating procedure (SOP). But now he realized that his own tank crew had not prepared a range card, at least not that he had seen. A review of his own range card would have told him that he was outside effective range of his own tank. Not only had he not checked range cards, but they were not added digitally to the Blue Force Tracker. Once again, he could have taken advantage of the skills of SFC Schnell to conduct precombat inspections of range cards, sector sketches, and defensive positions constructed by the engineers.

Worse yet, CPT Morris now recalled a point that one of his MCCC instructors had belabored to his small group. His words now hauntingly echoed: "You can learn a lot about your engagement area development by driving the engagement area from the enemy's perspective." Now CPT Morris thought to himself, "What if I had taken the time to drive the engagement area? Would I have discovered these issues? Could I have better identified dead space? Would I have seen the problems with covering the obstacles with fires?" He knew the answers. He certainly would have uncovered some of these glaring issues.

> **POINT: Company/team commanders and platoon leaders must develop engagement areas when organizing a defense. Obstacles have a designed purpose. Obstacles must be covered with fires by positioning direct-fire weapons and planning supporting fires such as artillery, attack aviation, and close air support.**

Perhaps CPT Morris also would have noticed the Bolcavian platoon attached to Team Anvil that was now to the left and in front of his adjusted battle position. He recalled Team Anvil reporting that it was taking fire from the rear area that destroyed one of the platoon's T-72 main battle tanks. Now he realized that, in the midst of the advancing enemy, his own team easily could have mistaken the T-72 for an enemy tank. He hoped it was not the case that his team had indeed fired on the Bolcavians. But there was a knot in his stomach as he realized it was likely.

> **POINT: In a modern decisive action environment involving multinational partners, it is at least possible, if not likely, that our partners are equipped with vehicles and systems similar to those of an enemy hybrid threat. Leaders must be diligent to prevent fratricide by mistaking friend for foe.**

Now CPT Morris gazed over the dusty, smoky engagement area, glancing at the small hill on the east side. In a retrospective moment of clarity, he realized what a perfect place that may have been to position Javelin teams on the reverse side. They would have been in ideal range to engage the lead mechanized vehicles as they entered the engagement area. There was a perfect concealed route to regress back to the main portion of the BP after initial engagement. It would have been easy to deploy teams into position from the BP, when the scouts reported and confirmed the avenue of approach and timing of the advancing enemy. This was undoubtedly a missed opportunity for Team Badger to set the conditions. As CPT Morris wandered past the first sergeant's heavily damaged vehicle, he noticed the thermal bore sight panel on the back. Now he tried to recall the last time they had driven the panel out to allow the crews to bore-sight. He knew the answer. They had not done so for days, and not since they had been in the BP. But these are the world's premier weapons systems. Did that really make a difference? He remembered the emphasis the O-C/Ts at NTC had placed on bore sighting. "But that was necessary just because of the MILES systems, right?" Maybe not. Now he thought he should have put more emphasis on the routine things.

POINT: Bore sighting and prefire checks must be part of unit SOPs and be enforced by leaders. Simple checklists in unit SOPs to assign and track responsibilities for priorities of work, combined with leader enforcement of standards, provide organization for efficiently and thoroughly preparing for combat.

CPT Morris' thoughts returned to the battle again. As the Apache helicopters had come on station, he had gained renewed hope to turn the tide in Team Badger's favor. But valuable time was wasted trying to gain communication with the attack helicopters. He recalled the initial transmission on the net.

"Badger 6, this is Blackhorse 21."

He had responded: "Blackhorse, clear the net. This an internal net!"

At the time he could not figure out who had broken into his team's command net. He was furiously trying to direct his crumbling team, and some joker was breaking in. After several transmissions to his platoon leaders, the call came again.

"Badger 6, this is Blackhorse 21. Apache team of two aircraft on station. Request direction, over."

All of a sudden, it hit him. He recalled the S-3 briefing the plan to push attack helicopters to team command nets for direct support. With the interruption of the task force command net, he must have missed the call that they were being pushed to his net. He had to get them in the fight. He had already wasted precious time.

"Badger 6, this is Blackhorse 21. Can you mark front line trace?"

Now CPT Morris realized he had not even thought about how to identify his positions to the aircraft. With the Blue Force Tracker net being jammed, the pilots could not rely on that to identify friendly locations. After several minutes of scrambling coordination with his platoon leaders, SFC Ellingson, the platoon sergeant from 4th Platoon, one of his Bradley platoons, was able to employ green smoke, marking the farthest east of Team Badger's position.

"Blackhorse 21, this is Badger 6. Green smoke marks farthest east of friendly position. Can you identify vehicles to the east?"

"Badger 6, this is Blackhorse 21, roger. Are we clear to engage?"

"Roger, cleared to engage targets east of green smoke."

CPT Morris knew this was haphazard coordination, at best. He had not identified specific targets. Sure, the Apaches were able to destroy three vehicles before they departed, but his platoons were engaging the same targets at the same time. If only he could have directed the attack helicopters to specific targets to supplement his direct fires and eliminate threats that were not already under fire. He had not really thought about where, when, and how to use the aviation assets until they were on the net. He sighed at what might have been, disappointed in himself for not including the Apaches in his defense plan.

By that time, the enemy lead elements had breached the main obstacles in the engagement area and were administering devastating direct-fire effects on his dwindling platoons. Although the FSO, 1LT Hearn, had planned fires supporting the obstacles, artillery fires were too late to affect the breaching forces. They had missed the opportunity. CPT Morris glanced at the disfigured Bradley Fire Support Team vehicle (B-FiST). He had worked the vehicle into his battle position for additional firepower. But now, as he looked at the B-FiST, he wondered if the FSO would have been able to observe the established triggers to fire the targets. "Probably not," he thought to himself. "Was anybody else responsible for the targets?" If CPT Morris did not know, who did? The infantry platoon forward observers would not have been able to identify the trigger, either, because of their positions. But 1LT Harris, one of his tank platoon leaders, was in position to identify the enemy lead elements first. "Did he know the targets and triggers?" CPT Morris knew that was not covered in the team rehearsals and only the FSO had participated in the task force fire-support rehearsal. CPT Morris shook his head in disappointment at having placed all of his proverbial fire support eggs in a single basket, that of 1LT Hearn. Then he wondered if the issues with attack aviation were discussed during the fires rehearsal. He did not know. He had not participated.

> **POINT:** "Rehearsals allow leaders and their Soldiers to practice key aspects of the concept of operations. These actions help Soldiers orient themselves to their environment and other units before executing the operation. Rehearsals help Soldiers build a lasting mental picture of the sequence of key actions within the operation." (Field Manual 6-0, *Commander and Staff Organization and Operations*, Chapter 12)

As the last of his wounded Soldiers were evacuated, CPT Morris recalled the moment Team Dagger arrived. With a well-placed artillery smoke screen obscuring its counterattack, Team Dagger maneuvered on the enemy, now nearly through the engagement area and closing on the BP. By that point, the FM communications had just returned to normal. Artillery fires rained on the softer enemy targets as Team Dagger's direct fires focused on the now-emerging enemy mechanized vehicles, tanks, and BMP infantry fighting vehicles. Fortunately, Team Badger had not encountered the mechanized forces early in the battle, or there would have been even bigger trouble. Almost on cue, Apaches were back on station and providing similarly devastating effects on the enemy. And then the close air support (CAS) arrived. As if the timing were scripted, the CAS, artillery, attack aviation, and maneuver direct fires tore through the attacking enemy formations.

Despite Team Dagger's success in stopping the enemy attack, Team Badger suffered devastating losses. It now consisted of only four operational combat vehicles and 17 personnel who were not killed or wounded. How had this gone so horribly wrong?

Background

Task Force Mustang had spent the past two months conducting stability operations in the city of Voloslav in the small European country of Bolcavia. The country, and its scattered communities, had struggled for the past 15 years after declaring independence from Arcania. Bolcavia's governmental structure, military, and economy were immature and still developing. Growing pains were evident as the people struggled to gain their collective cultural identity as an independent nation. Although the majority of the population supported independence and developed a sense of pride and patriotism toward the newly established separate nation, there was still a large contingent that held loyalties to Arcania and were Bolcavian merely by geographic location, not governmental loyalty.

While the national government struggled to gain identity as it conducted major functions, such as establishing international trade, specifying domestic policies, and building national defense systems, day-to-day life carried on, for the most part. People remained where they had lived their entire lives. Their children attended the same schools. Churches, social gatherings, and customs remained predominantly the same as they were prior to independence. However, during the past three years, a growing contingent of separatists had organized, gained significant financial support, and were now backed by Arcania. The former governing power was known to be providing training and equipment to an ever-increasing and robust separatist force, whose political statements warned of reclaiming Bolcavia under the rule of Arcania. There was even evidence that as many as 4,000 regular military soldiers from Arcania were augmenting these separatist forces. If true, this would be significant because it would nearly double the separatists' size and capability. Indications were that they were being equipped and trained with the latest technology developed by Arcania, which meant near-peer capability compared to current Western forces. Six months ago, the separatists conducted an organized attack against Bolcavian forces, indicating that their formations were now very capable of posing a significant threat to national security and were continuing to gain momentum.

In addition to these conventional forces, several organized criminal elements were scattered throughout Bolcavia. These loosely organized elements, although not great in number, were increasingly disrupting local commerce, and their levels of audacity and intimidation continued to rise, even to the point of conducting indiscriminate terrorist-style attacks on population centers. The city of Voloslav was a particular target for these criminal and terrorist organizations because of its economic and political importance. Now there was evidence that criminal organizations were collaborating with the conventional separatist forces, coordinating attacks particularly aimed at weakening Bolcavia's defense forces. U.S. forces had identified, and were tracking, several social media accounts that were used in coordinating these attacks. It was apparent that social media communications occurred among criminal, terrorist, and conventional forces.

Bolcavia, with a population of 34 million, maintained a military of just under 100,000, including a navy of about 5,000, an air force of 32,000, and an army of 61,000. Upon gaining independence, Bolcavia inherited troops and equipment that had been part of the Arcanian military. The force consisted mainly of former Soviet equipment and relied on Cold War-era training and tactics. However, upon gaining independence, Bolcavia sought partnership with Western nations, specifically NATO countries. Now the new nation has integrated equipment from Britain, France, and the United States and has developed training relationships designed to modernize the structure, training, tactics, and leadership of its forces. However, these programs are still in a stage of relative infancy, and the defense forces are only moderately capable of deterring threats to national security.

As internal threats, supported by external funding and forces, became apparent, Bolcavia appealed for assistance from its newly acquired allies in maintaining stability in the country and region. A coalition was formed, and member forces deployed in support of Bolcavia. The majority of coalition forces came from the United States, including a division capable of sustained operations and integrating joint enablers. The U.S. Air Force, Navy, and Marine Corps provided substantial support to the mission. Britain, France, Australia, and Canada also provided ground forces, joined by a smattering of smaller contingencies from other nations providing tactical and logistic support to the mission. The U.S. division headquarters served as a joint task force headquarters. A combined joint task force multinational command, under which all coalition forces operated, was established in Germany.

Task Force Mustang operated under the command of the 2nd Brigade Combat Team (2BCT) in Area of Operations Voloslav. Amid indications of a planned attack by the separatist forces, 2BCT was transitioning to combined arms maneuver after having spent the past two months largely focused on stability operations in wide area security.

POINT: The U.S. Army Chief of Staff defined a hybrid threat in 2008 as an adversary that incorporates "diverse and dynamic combinations of conventional, irregular, terrorist, and criminal capabilities." No two threats are alike. It is important to understand and account for enemy assets and capabilities in specific environments.

Task Force Mustang
Tactical Operations Center
H-66 Hours (1200L)

LTC Milner's staff had diligently prepared a detailed operation order (OPORD) for the assembled team commanders. But in the back of his mind he knew that, regardless of the hard work and dedication of his staff, there certainly would be some aspect that they had not addressed adequately or at all. He was looking forward to the feedback from his team commanders during back briefs and as they conducted their own mission preparation. He knew the next three days would fly by and wanted to make sure he had done everything he could to set the conditions for the success of the task force. He felt pretty good about his staff's work to this point.

As CPT Glenn Robinson, the task force S-2, laid out the enemy situation for the commanders, CPT Morris paid particular attention to the anticipated avenues of approach and formations of the enemy brigade. Knowing from the warning order that retaining the key terrain in Team Badger's battle position (BP) was the Task Force Mustang decisive operation, CPT Morris felt that the most important task was to destroy the handful of enemy mechanized forces, tanks, and BMP infantry fighting vehicles organized among the hodgepodge brigade that CPT Robinson compared to the motorized rifle regiments seen years ago. He noted the S-2 indicated that the most likely avenue of approach led directly into Engagement Area Blackjack and that the lead motorized rifle battalion contained the bulk of the tanks and BMPs the brigade had in its formation.

CPT Morris was certain that if his team could eliminate the enemy mechanized assets, the task force would cruise to easy victory over the remainder of the motorized brigade. The combat power of M1s and M2s seriously overmatched the other equipment of the brigade. As the S-2 continued through the enemy situation, CPT Morris' mind wandered to his initial plan to establish his BP and focus his efforts on destroying those tanks and BMPs.

Meanwhile, CPT Crafton listened attentively to the detailed layout of the intelligence preparation of the battlefield (IPB) that CPT Robinson had so diligently studied and portrayed to the team commanders. CPT Crafton's ears perked up as CPT Robinson mentioned the possibility of Arcanian electronic warfare jamming assets potentially integrated into the formation. The S-2 also mentioned there was intelligence leading the BCT S-2 to believe that Arcanian aviation assets were positioned near the Bolcavian border and could potentially support the attacking forces. CPT Robinson mentioned the unmanned aircraft system (UAS) capability, already used by the separatist force, and indicated that the BCT air defense officer was

19

working the counter-UAS threat, but that the task force could assume it was under observation by enemy UAS assets. He also mentioned there had been several instances throughout the BCT and division areas in which terrorist mortar attacks against U.S. forces and the Bolcavian population had been preceded by the presence of quadcopters, the kind popular among civilians as a hobby. CPT Robinson said the terrorist attacks and the presence of these quadcopters indicated that there were terrorist or criminal organizations using these drones as surveillance and reconnaissance devices. Criminal and terrorist organizations had become increasingly capable of building and emplacing improvised explosive devices, continually refining their technology and tactics, techniques, and procedures. Finally, CPT Robinson mentioned that, during previous operations, the separatist forces had intentionally occupied village residences and displaced civilians from their homes. Doing so provided them with resources and established a sort of sanctuary, making it difficult for coalition forces to target them among the civilian population. Additionally, occupying civilian residences caused Bolcavian and coalition forces to expend their resources in dealing with the resulting displaced population.

CPT Crafton homed in on many of the details provided in the S-2's very thorough brief. He needed to make sure he accounted for threat characteristics in his planning. He knew that Team Dagger, being designated the task force reserve, would be a critical part of the decisive operation during the counterattack, whenever and wherever that might occur.

At the conclusion of the staff's OPORD brief, LTC Milner took the opportunity to address his team commanders again. "I know I gave you my intent, but I want to reiterate to ensure everybody is clear. I anticipate there will be times when communication is disrupted or there is confusion on the battlefield. Each of you needs to be able to make decisions and execute within my intent. You all have a copy of my commander's critical information requirements and the decision support matrix in the order. Those are the critical events that I see occurring during the battle. The staff and I will be evaluating it as the IPB develops. I need your feedback based on your preparations."

He paused a moment to gauge the attentiveness of his team commanders. Satisfied that they understood the importance, he continued: "The purpose of this defense is to deny the enemy access to Voloslav. We absolutely cannot allow an enemy force, of platoon size or greater, to get into the city. Ideally, no enemy forces reach the city at all. I see the initial defense setting the conditions for a potential counterattack by the task force reserve, and that is what I see as the decisive operation. Timing and location for commitment of the reserve are critical. We must be able to identify the enemy's mechanized assets, his most formidable combat systems. If we commit too early, we may allow him to bring his tanks and BMPs to bear against our counterattack. Keep in mind that we are fighting an intelligent and adaptive enemy, and we may need to commit the reserve to deny penetration of our defense before the mechanized forces engage. I want to be prepared to seize the initiative with a counterattack, but at the same time, also be prepared to supplement any of the team battle positions. Captain Crafton, are you clear on the anticipated triggers for each of these options?"

"Yes, Sir," he replied. "If mechanized forces get beyond the initial obstacles in any of the team engagement areas, we will attack to destroy those forces while still in the engagement areas. If any of the teams reach 60 percent combat power or below, I need to be prepared to supplement their defenses."

"Right. I anticipate making that decision," LTC Milner added, "but if you see that these conditions are met, and you have not heard from me, I don't want you to hesitate and miss the window. It could mean the difference between success and failure."

"Yes, Sir. If I identify conditions are met, I will immediately come up on the net for a decision. In the event there is no response, I will execute within your intent."

> **POINT: In exercising mission command, commanders must be able to understand, visualize, describe, and direct operations to seize the initiative over the enemy and accomplish the mission. Subordinate leaders must ensure they clearly understand the commander's intent in order to operate under the philosophy of mission command. It is crucial that the commander give enough of a framework that subordinate leaders know what to do, when to do it, and why it is being done.**

LTC Milner knew he had selected the right commander for the critical mission of task force reserve. All of his commanders were competent and talented young leaders with unique attributes, but CPT Crafton stood out as an agile and adaptive leader. He was a team player, always seeing the big picture of the task force and putting that success ahead of his team's success. In developing a capable task force formation, CPT Crafton's team was a key element. He was thorough, calculating, and collected under pressure. LTC Milner knew that if all went to hell in a handbasket, he could count on CPT Crafton to make timely decisions with calculated judgment. "He's going to be a battalion commander one day," LTC Milner thought.

As the meeting was breaking up, CPT Crafton caught LTC Milner in the corner of the tactical operations center (TOC). It seemed he was always the one who cornered the boss to ask to clarify any point. The other commanders teased him about it. He heard CPT Morris mumble "teacher's pet" under his breath. He saw CPT Juan Hernandez, the Team Cobra commander, and CPT Li Wang, the Team Anvil commander, pointing and smirking as he approached LTC Milner. CPT Crafton knew the others thought he lacked confidence when he always ran to the commander to go over the plan after any briefing. Even in garrison, after training meetings, he wanted to ensure he clearly understood the boss' intent. He did not care what the others thought. He was a critical part of the decisive operation of the task force, and success depended on how he executed his mission. There were a lot of moving pieces, and he wanted to make sure he got it all right.

"Sir, I understand the criteria for committing the reserve, but I wanted to get your thoughts on something. If the mechanized forces are identified and there is simultaneously an enemy penetration of one of the team defensive positions, how do you feel about committing a platoon to supplement a defensive position and retaining the remainder of Team Dagger as a reserve, maintaining capability for a counterattack?"

LTC Milner smiled. He had thought about that himself. He was even more confident now that CPT Crafton was on the same page. He called MAJ Jorge Santiago, the battalion operations officer, over to the discussion.

"Major Santiago, remember discussing potentially splitting the reserve during war gaming?" "Yes, Sir. We discussed that as a possible decision point," MAJ Santiago replied.

"Well, I want you to flesh out the details of that decision point. Establish specific criteria for that contingency and assign appropriate commander's critical information requirements for collection. Get the S-2 to add it to his collection plan. Criteria should address one or more points of enemy penetration and simultaneous identification of mechanized forces in an engagement area. This could affect any of the company/teams, so ensure all the commanders are tracking any updates, too. Captain Crafton, what were you thinking if we decide to do this?"

The captain gathered his thoughts for a moment, then replied, "Sir, I'd identify Fourth Platoon, a Bradley platoon, as a potential back stop to supplement a team defensive position. Lieutenant Steve Warrington is the platoon leader. He's my most experienced and reliable platoon leader. I would stay with the bulk of the team and I would retain the tank platoons, because they would be the most beneficial once the team is mobile during a counterattack."

"That's what I thought you would say." LTC Milner smiled again. He had thought the very same thing for the same reasons. "Major Santiago, add that to the decision support template. Let's discuss this during the task force rehearsal. Keep Captain Crafton and the other commanders up to date on any additional details and updates to the decision support matrix."

> **POINT: Agile and adaptive leaders are capable of critical thinking and problem solving, resulting in creative solutions to complex problems.**

LTC Milner knew MAJ Santiago was a thorough, detailed planner, one of the best he had seen. He also knew that CPT Crafton and MAJ Santiago worked fantastically together. He had seen it during home station training and at the National Training Center. CPT Crafton continually provided feedback to MAJ Santiago on the task force plans. And MAJ Santiago regularly sought CPT Crafton's perspective as a company commander. There was very apparent mutual respect. The captain admired the major for the planner and leader that he was. The major valued the candor and critical feedback he received from the captain. LTC Milner was confident that between MAJ Santiago and CPT Crafton, this possible contingency would be adequately addressed.

CPT Crafton had another question. "Sir, I see that I've got an attached route clearance team from the brigade engineer battalion. I was hoping that I could link up with them ASAP so I can ensure they are integrated in the planning and rehearsals with the team."

"Staff Sergeant Harris and his crew are waiting for you now to go back with you." LTC Milner knew the importance of integrating attachments early for the very reasons CPT Crafton had mentioned.

"Sir," the captain continued, "I'm concerned about communication during the battle. The S-2 discussed the enemy's electronic warfare assets. I also noticed the EW system was on the fire support officer's high-payoff target list. But the target synchronization matrix only identified Team Badger as a primary shooter with no alternates. I also thought this might be a target we could nominate to brigade for an armed UAS strike, if identified."

"Wow!" LTC Milner thought. Neither he nor his staff had even considered the possibility of nominating targets to brigade for an armed UAS attack. Now CPT Crafton was really demonstrating his prowess as a commander.

"Captain Wilson, come here." LTC Milner summoned his task force fire support officer, who hurried over. "Captain Crafton just had an idea about targeting the enemy EW systems. Tell him, Gerald."

After CPT Crafton explained his suggestion, LTC Milner said, "Captain Wilson, go through the high-payoff target list and the target synchronization matrix and ensure we've identified primary and alternate delivery systems as well as primary and alternate observers. Consider assets that brigade has to help us identify and attack enemy targets on the HPTL. Get those requests in ASAP."

"Got it, Sir." CPT Wilson turned to return to his fire support element to begin going over those details.

"FSO, wait." CPT Crafton stopped him. There was something else. He turned back to LTC Milner: "Sir, I also didn't hear anything in the order about our own EW. The S-2 briefed that the enemy was relying a lot on cellphone communication, particularly between the conventional and irregular components. It seems like we could take that away from them."

"Captain Wilson, see what brigade has available and what we can request through division. I want to block cellphones, at a minimum, as the enemy enters the engagement area."

CPT Wilson hurried to his M577 command post vehicle, which held the fire support element, to get busy. He was disappointed that he had not thought of those things. He had been too focused on field artillery to consider nonlethal fires. Now he started to question if he had spent enough time synchronizing aviation and close air support into the fight. He needed to get busy, fast.

> **POINT: Consider assets at higher echelons that bring combat power to bear on the enemy.**

"Sir," CPT Crafton continued, "if we do block cellphones, it most likely will affect the people in Voloslav. If you remember the last time that happened, it caused quite a stir and we had a lot of people angry. I would suggest brigade be ready with a message explaining why that happened and why it was important. It could prevent the backlash we saw last time. Also, I got a visit from Councilman Dmytro Kravchuk. He wanted to know why we had suddenly left the city. He felt that we were abandoning his people and leaving them vulnerable to the criminal elements in the city. I assured him that one battalion from the brigade was remaining in the city to maintain stability, but that we needed to address a potential conventional threat. He seemed to understand, but I think a message that informed people in Voloslav that the brigade is still here to support them could go a long way toward reassurance. We could also inform them that the separatists are planning operations and ask them to avoid the main battle area, without disclosing too much detail. At the same time, brigade could establish a hotline and ask the people to report any suspicious activity that appears to be coordinated with the separatist elements. Brigade could identify and address those problems early. We know that the enemy has employed special operations forces early in its operations before. The people will probably be the first to notice those activities. We could enlist their support."

LTC Milner was blown away. This was seriously advanced analysis and terrific recommendations from CPT Crafton. He made a note to get with the brigade S-3 and information operations officer on these very things. He would take these on personally. He needed his staff to focus on the main battle area. He would coordinate with the brigade staff for these issues. Why hadn't he thought about information operations (IO)? He needed to review the latest themes and messages from brigade. They probably needed to be updated and he wanted to ensure his task force was aligned and nested with appropriate brigade messages. Now that he thought about it, he probably should give the mayor a call.

CPT Crafton continued, "Sir, as close as we are to the city and as likely as civilians from other towns and cities are to flee as the enemy advances, I'm not comfortable with our ability to deal with civilians on the battlefield efficiently. Sure, we can designate teams to direct civilians, but we could certainly use brigade support to allow us to focus on the conventional forces. Based on my initial assessment, I recommend directing the civilians here." CPT Crafton indicated on his map a route that bypassed planned obstacles and led to a safe collection point, from which civilians could be evacuated from the task force defensive position and engagement area.

LTC Milner had already discussed this very thing with the BCT commander moments before the OPORD briefing began. Brigade was developing a concept and support package to assist with potential civilian refugees on the battlefield.

"Brigade is working on that, and the staff should have an update tomorrow on the plan for potential refugees or civilians we may encounter on the battlefield," LTC Milner replied.

> **POINT: Integration of nonlethal means, such as electronic warfare, cyber operations, public affairs, civil affairs, and information operations, are important considerations in synchronization. Consider the effects on civilian populations as well as friendly and enemy forces while executing the Army's core competencies of combined arms maneuver and wide area security through decisive action.**

"Roger, Sir. Finally, I think the plan for primary and alternate communications, using FM command net and Blue Force Tracker, is fine. But I'm worried about contingency or emergency means of communication. I'm thinking of identifying a vehicle runner to the task force TOC from Team Dagger in case FM and satellite communications are disrupted. It would be a way to maintain communication if necessary. Also, I think visual signals, such as star clusters, may be a last-resort emergency means to communicate."

LTC Milner called his signal officer, 1LT Tim Holmes, to the discussion. "Lieutenant Holmes, I want you to coordinate with Team Dagger and the other teams to work out contingency and emergency communications to the TOC. Ensure we have coordinated means for emergency communication. That means establishing signals and ensuring the teams have pyrotechnics on hand as appropriate. Get with the S-4 and the teams ASAP to see what we have on hand. Brief me on the tentative plan in two hours, and be prepared to discuss during rehearsals and any updates with the commanders."

> **POINT: Plan primary, alternate, contingency, and emergency (PACE) means for communications and other systems. Have redundant systems in place, and rehearse their use.**

Satisfied that his concerns had been addressed, for now, CPT Crafton went to see CPT Robinson, the S-2. After reviewing and confirming the IPB as briefed in the order, CPT Crafton asked, "Do you have photos of the enemy EW system? I don't know that our Soldiers are familiar with it, and want them to know what it looks like."

"Sure, we have some photos from the UAS and ones that were taken on the ground with civilian cellphones that we got through open-source means. Let me print them for you."

CPT Crafton got two good, clear photos, one aerial and one ground. "So that's what this thing looks like," he thought to himself. It should be easy to identify with all of the antennas on the vehicle. But if he was just now seeing it for the first time, his NCOs and Soldiers probably have not seen it. He needed to make sure all of them were familiar with this system. He made several copies to distribute through the team.

> **POINT: Visual identification of enemy vehicles and assets is critical. Soldiers must be familiar with, and able to distinguish between, enemy and friendly forces. Leverage available systems and capabilities for real-time enemy visual products.**

CPT Crafton knew he would have more concerns as he continued planning and preparation, but for now he needed to get back to Team Dagger. He needed to get things going. Time was ticking.

Team Dagger
Tactical Assembly Area
H-62 Hours (1800L)

During the ride back to the Team Dagger command post, CPT Crafton carefully studied the map. In particular, he looked at the most likely and most dangerous avenues of approach that the S-2 had identified. Keeping in mind that the purpose of the defense was to deny enemy entry into Voloslav, he noticed another potential avenue to the city that the S-2 had not addressed. This route would potentially bypass the task force defensive positions. He needed to see it on the ground to determine if this was a valid concern.

His mind also wandered over the home station training leading up to deployment, including the National Training Center (NTC) rotation that had been so demanding. He recalled the training package that the Center for Army Lessons Learned (CALL) liaison officer had sent to the unit containing NTC decisive action training environment newsletters, combat training center observations, handbooks, and graphic training aids (GTAs). He had downloaded and printed several of the handbooks and GTAs from the CALL website to bring with him. Specifically, he recalled his own unit's lessons learned that were reflected in after action reviews from the NTC. Just before deployment he had reviewed them on the Joint Lessons Learned Information System (JLLIS). He did not want to let anything slip through the cracks, and he certainly did not want to repeat any of the mistakes his unit had made during training. Most importantly, he was going through the SOP checklist for priorities of work per standard operating procedure (SOP). Team Dagger had validated the usefulness of this checklist at the NTC. It was a very valuable tool to organize his planning efforts.

POINT: Knowledge and lessons learned information are valuable only if accessed and applied in training and combat. Lessons learned; tactics, techniques, and procedures; and best practices are readily available at the CALL website, JLLIS, the Army Training Network (ATN), warfighting forums, and combat training center (National Training Center, Joint Regional Training Center, and Joint Multinational Readiness Center) websites, among others.

CPT Crafton called his executive officer, 1LT Mike Loggins, instructing him to gather the first sergeant, fire support officer (FSO), platoon leaders, and platoon sergeants. He wanted to give a quick warning order to allow them to begin preparation while he finalized his plan for a more thorough order. He also told the XO to get SGT Masters and SPC Waring from the company headquarters. SGT Masters, who also served as the chemical, biological, radiological, and nuclear NCO, had shown particular interest in and a special knack for intelligence stuff. SPC Waring had developed that same knack. CPT Crafton knew they had primary jobs, but their value in other aspects was tremendous. He wanted to brief them on the intelligence preparation of the battlefield and have them get started on a terrain model to be used for team rehearsals. He had other thoughts about how to use their skills, but that could wait for now. CPT Crafton knew his team faced an adaptive enemy in a complex environment. He understood that it is the commander's responsibility to conduct additional, more detailed analysis of his area of operations to provide the detail necessary to his subordinate elements.

After giving a quick briefing to his leaders and answering their initial questions, CPT Crafton gave some specific instructions to his leaders. "Although we are in a role that requires us to be mobile, we still need to make every effort to protect the team from enemy threats. We need to consider survivability to be ready to move into the fight. I am particularly concerned about enemy air and artillery threats. Make sure your people and equipment are adequately protected. Pay attention to camouflage, particularly to avoid detection by unmanned aerial system assets. Assume somebody is looking. We also need to pay attention to reducing our electronic signature. The enemy's electronic warfare capabilities leave us more vulnerable to detection and disruption of our electronic systems. We need to maintain electronic signature discipline."

> **POINT: In avoiding enemy detection, consider concealment from ground and air assets. In addition to visual concealment, consider how to minimize detection of electronic signatures through technology discipline and masking. Consider the enemy's capability for electronic acquisition and apply appropriate countermeasures.**

CPT Crafton knew his leaders understood, and he could see they were ready to get going. He ran down a timeline for coming events, including a detailed orders brief, leader route recons, and rehearsals. He assigned responsibilities for priorities of work to the platoons and issued guidance to the first sergeant, executive officer, FSO, and master gunner in accordance with the unit SOP. He thought to himself: "The plan goes so much smoother when I challenge subordinate leaders based on their strengths and expertise. I have really great officers and NCOs in Headquarters Platoon to assist with precombat inspections, rehearsals, sand tables, and specific sections of my operation order. The leaders in each of the tank and infantry platoons always come through, too."

"I'll see you back in three hours. Lieutenant Warrington, hang around for a minute. I want to give you some specific instructions."

The other leaders dispersed. On the way out, 1SG Young shouted over to the medics. CPT Crafton knew the first sergeant would take care of the troops by paying attention to the myriad intangible details. They had been down this road, and Top already knew what to do. He would have the medics taking care of any issues his Soldiers had. Also, 1SG would coordinate things like mail runs and chow schedules. Inevitably, Team Dagger would have the best possible care and provisions. Top had already met SSG Harris and the brigade engineering battalion route clearance team and had them staged in the assembly area. CPT Crafton heard 1SG Young call to update his troop strength to the S-1, also accounting for additional meals and provisions for the attached crew. CPT Crafton didn't have to say a word. If he knew 1SG Young, he probably had already scheduled a visit from the chaplain, too. CPT Crafton smiled. A first sergeant like that was a tremendously valuable asset.

The commander told 1LT Warrington: "The task force may decide to split a platoon from the team, if we need to supplement another team defense with a smaller force. If that happens, your platoon is the one I will send. You need to be familiar with all routes to all team battle positions. You also need to coordinate with each team in case you need to link up during battle. That will be time intensive. As your platoon starts preparations, I want you to start your route recon. Link up with each team commander and know their plans and positions. If Team Dagger is committed to any of the team battle positions as a whole, you will be my lead platoon. I also need you to report back to me on any refinements to the teams' positions or engagement areas. I'll do my own recon later, but I need you to get going right away. Any questions?"

"No, Sir. Based on your brief, I anticipated this was coming. I'm on it."

CPT Crafton nodded. He would get planning his order, but he was relying on reconnaissance feedback from 1LT Warrington before he could complete his plan and issue the operation order to the company. He was not going to just rely on the intelligence preparation of the battlefield (IPB) from the S-2 based on a map reconnaissance. It needed refinement, and he owed CPT Robinson feedback to help develop the IPB. He knew 1LT Warrington would come through.

> **POINT: Prepare and rehearse for the range of options available to the commander. The ability to rapidly implement contingency plans gives the commander options to apply combat power.**

Team Dagger
Tactical Assembly Area
H-59 Hours (2100L)

Team Dagger leaders gathered right on time for CPT Crafton to issue his order. The commander was pleased with the terrain model that SGT Masters and SPC Waring had constructed. His platoon leaders and noncommissioned officers gathered around the model that depicted the array of battle positions (BPs) in the task force and the Team Dagger assembly area. SGT Masters and SPC Waring had anticipated the darkness and constructed a shelter over the terrain model, large enough to accommodate the leaders and lights. Now this model could be used day or night and still maintain light discipline.

The 4th Platoon leader, 1LT Warrington, had returned just before the group gathered and had filled in some valuable information on the routes to the battle positions. He had taken SSG Harris with him so he could get an idea of any potential route clearance issues. They informed the captain of what they had learned on the recon. 1LT Warrington also indicated that Team Badger had shifted the location of its battle position from where it was initially planned by the task force. CPT Crafton updated the locations on the terrain model. He noticed it left a considerable gap between Team Badger and Team Cobra, one that the enemy could exploit if it breaches initial obstacles in the engagement area. He made a mental note to talk with CPT Morris, the Team Badger commander, about his plan during his recon of the routes and positions later.

At the conclusion of the orders brief, CPT Crafton emphasized his concerns to his leaders. "It is critical that we all maintain situational awareness as the battle develops. We have to be able to use initiative to meet the task force commander's intent. We need to be able to identify critical events on the battlefield. We could potentially support any of the other three teams in the task force. We need to be familiar with each of their BPs, the routes to each, and each team's defensive plan. We have to coordinate link-up procedures with each and be ready for a variety of scenarios, depending on how the battle unfolds.

"I am concerned about protecting our team during the initial stages of the battle. The other teams have priority of engineer assets during construction of their battle positions. The enemy has the capability to observe our preparation and will almost certainly use air and artillery to precede their attack. We cannot afford to lose combat power before we get into the fight. We have to use concealment from both ground and air observation. We will move into our alternate assembly area before the enemy gains contact. Make sure you spend time preparing those positions.

"We will conduct route recons in both day and night to ensure we can react with timeliness. We will rehearse contingencies, and we have quite a few possible alternatives. Our first route recon will be tomorrow morning. We will have a sand table rehearsal with key leaders prior to dark and will conduct night recons after dark. We need to ensure force protection by securing the terrain on our flanks. To our east and west we have several covered and concealed passes where the enemy can attack undetected. First Platoon, you need to make sure you identify enemy avenues of approach and dead space on the eastern flank. Second Platoon, you do the same on the western flank. We have to maintain 360-degree security at all times, whether in the assembly area or preparing positions. Once we ensure we have no enemy observers seeing our activities, we need to maintain our own observation posts to ensure the terrain remains clear and provide early warning. Report the locations of your OPs, flank security, and infantry squad positions when you turn in your refined sector sketches to the master gunner. He will help me with the direct-fire plan.

"Fire Support Officer, you need to be integrated into any changes the platoon leaders report. Plan targets on potential avenues of approach as identified. Calculate triggers for observers to call fires based on the enemy rate of movement. Provide an updated fire support matrix, and we will share it with task force. Get with the task force FSO and the other team FSOs. Make sure we have all the refined targets from the other teams as they develop engagement areas. Disseminate down to the platoon leaders and forward observers.

"We all need to be on the same page. We need to identify any maintenance and supply issues right away. Ensure we follow the SOP for precombat checks and inspections. I'll be around to spot-check, as usual. I know you all know what to do. Let's make sure we do not let anything slip through the cracks. I plan to issue a fragmentary order within two hours after platoon leaders provide information from your infantry squad's reconnaissance. Any questions?"

Seeing that his leaders were anxious to continue preparation, and satisfied that they understood his intent, CPT Crafton retreated to his vehicle to grab something to eat and perhaps a 15-minute power nap. He knew the next couple of days were going to be physically, mentally, and emotionally demanding on him and his Soldiers. He needed to ensure he took care of himself to maintain his physical and mental readiness.

Team Dagger
Tactical Assembly Area
H-48 Hours (0600L)

The leaders of Team Dagger assembled right on time in the alternate assembly area to conduct the route recon to the battle positions. This was CPT Crafton's first chance to see the preparations of the assembly area. He was satisfied so far. He had coordinated with the task force S-3 to expand the designated assembly area from the initial planned location. This allowed Team Dagger to disperse platoons and individual vehicles to protect against loss of significant combat power to potential enemy fires. Yet they were still located within close enough proximity to execute tactical movement from the assembly area to any of the battle positions (BPs) quickly and orderly, should the need arise, and maintain security against potential attacks from improvised explosive devices, snipers, or other criminal or terrorist elements.

Once all were ready, CPT Crafton gave some quick instructions. "We need to be very familiar with the routes both in daylight and darkness. We also need to understand our scheme of maneuver along those routes, where potential positions of cover and concealment may be, areas of potential exposure and risk to enemy forces, where we can take advantage of massing fires against the enemy in engagement areas, and any potential obstacles or restrictions we may encounter."

"Sir, we do have Blue Force Tracker," SSG Molina from 3rd Platoon chimed in. "It really isn't that hard to follow the routes on BFT."

"Yes, but...," CPT Crafton snapped back, "we need to not only follow the routes, but maintain our tactical formations. Also, we need to assume the worst and expect that BFTs may not be available. Remember the jamming assets the enemy has. We must be ready for worst-case scenarios."

SSG Molina slumped and hung his head a little. He knew better than that. The commander was right. They had all been through this before. Of course the BFTs had never failed during the National Training Center rotation prior to deployment. But SSG Molina knew this was different. He knew CPT Crafton was correct in paying attention to all possible situations. He knew Team Dagger was better for this attention to detail.

POINT: Rehearse in daylight and darkness, and replicate the range of conditions in degraded operations during rehearsals.

CPT Crafton continued: "I know you all know Staff Sergeant Harris and his crew by now. They will be an integral part of clearing routes for us prior to commitment. Make sure your crews understand the clearance team's task, purpose, and how they are integrated in our movement."

The commander briefed the team on which order it would recon the battle positions, starting with the most likely enemy situation, as briefed by the task force S-2, and working subsequently through the other two. He had already coordinated with each commander to get a quick brief on each team's BP and engagement area. He knew that was valuable time for the commanders during their preparations, but he also knew how critical that coordination would be if Team Dagger needed to link up with or pass through the teams. It could literally mean life or death for the Soldiers of Team Dagger or any of the other teams.

Once instructions were issued, Team Dagger moved out on reconnaissance. CPT Crafton halted the convoy at key locations along the route, each time orienting his leaders to the surrounding terrain and portraying his concept for the tactical maneuver through each location. The Raven operator, SGT Alvarez, launched and flew the company-level unmanned aerial system to provide an additional perspective, helping to identify potentially dangerous areas along the route. CPT Crafton explained his recommended noncombatant evacuation plan. He ensured his leaders understood that the locations were tentative, but that they needed to have a plan to quickly evacuate civilians from the battlefield. He would confirm the final plan with the tactical operations center (TOC). Although it was a slow and tedious process, CPT Crafton could see the understanding of the tactical mission continuing to develop in each of his leaders. It seemed painful now, but it would pay off in the long run.

Once the team arrived at BP Badger, CPT Crafton could see the flurry of work commencing in the battle position and the engagement area (EA). On one of the tanks, three Soldiers stood holding what appeared to be a smart phone and taking a selfie. He knew there should not be any cellphones with the Soldiers, but the first sergeant had confiscated one from one of his own Soldiers in Voloslav just three weeks ago, so he knew they were out there. With cell service readily available throughout Bolcavia, he also knew this was a potentially dangerous prospect. Additionally, he knew Soldiers would likely use their phones to send messages to their loved ones at home. Family members would then potentially post the information to social media, or otherwise share information, which could reach an exponentially wider audience. Operations security (OPSEC) could be compromised quickly.

CPT Crafton was glad he had dedicated time at home station to training his Soldiers on OPSEC and the use of social media. During a family readiness group meeting he also had briefed spouses on the dangers of sharing information about the deployment. He knew that technology and information were very difficult things to control, and he depended on his leaders to emphasize education and training of these issues. The commander hoped his efforts were not undermined by careless release of information by other teams. He would address that with CPT Morris before leaving BP Badger.

> **POINT: With ever-increasing technology, individuals have ever-increasing capabilities. Social media use is a particular OPSEC concern. Families and friends, not just Soldiers, must be aware of OPSEC and how to avoid providing information to potential enemy information collectors.**

CPT Morris strolled up from his command post (CP). "Hey, I forgot you guys were going to be here this morning. Give me a second to grab my map and I'll be right with you."

CPT Crafton was frustrated. He had deliberately coordinated each visit and was trying to maintain his timeline. It was already going to be a long day and he did not want to fall behind. He knew the other commanders were sacrificing their time for the scheduled updates and he did not want to disrupt their schedules.

CPT Morris was similarly frustrated. It seemed to him that CPT Crafton could obtain the updated graphics on BFT or from the S-3. Why did he need to use his valuable time to brief CPT Crafton's team?

SGT Alvarez flew the Raven over the BP and EA, and Team Dagger's leaders viewed the footage. This provided a better understanding of the terrain, vehicle fighting positions, and obstacle plan.

CPT Morris emerged from the CP with map and BP diagram in hand. He ran through the development of the EA and each of the fighting vehicle positions in his BP, describing his team's plan to the Team Dagger leaders. Viewing the Raven footage provided greater clarity of Team Badger's plan.

CPT Crafton then described Team Dagger's maneuver plan, should it be committed at BP Badger. He then asked about link-up procedures. CPT Morris frankly hadn't thought about that. After all, this battle should be won long before commitment of the reserve. He would get his executive officer to work out the link-up procedures.

"What about bypass routes through the obstacles in the EA?" CPT Crafton asked. CPT Morris pointed out the established bypass route and the markers Team Badger had emplaced to identify the route. He smugly grinned. "I bet Crafton didn't think I'd thought about that," he thought to himself.

"What fire control measures are in place if we should pass through your BP?" CPT Crafton continued.

CPT Morris' grin disappeared. He had not considered that. He and CPT Crafton quickly coordinated a restrictive fire line (RFL) based on the terrain through which Team Dagger would potentially pass and a readily identifiable water tower, just beyond the EA.

CPT Crafton was satisfied the control measure would be adequate. At the same time, he sure hoped that all of CPT Morris' leaders got the word and understood the RFL. If not, it could get ugly. CPT Morris agreed to report the RFL to the task force himself to be placed on the graphics. CPT Crafton made a mental note to follow up with MAJ Santiago, just to be sure.

> **POINT: Link-up and passage of lines are potentially dangerous operations. Units involved must coordinate closely. Routes and control measures must be established to prevent fratricide with obstacles or fires.**

After a few more minutes of discussion and coordination, CPT Crafton was satisfied that his leaders understood Team Badger's plan and position. He was ready to move on. Before leaving, he pulled CPT Morris aside and asked if he knew about his Soldiers with the cellphone. CPT Morris shrugged it off. He knew some of his Soldiers had managed to keep hold of their phones. It seemed harmless to him and was a sort of morale boost. It was a way to keep in touch with Families at home. He had deliberately ignored the cellphone issue. What harm could it really be? And all Soldiers knew they needed to maintain OPSEC, right?

CPT Crafton shook his head in disagreement. This would never be tolerated in Team Dagger. Not only was it a threat to OPSEC, it was an indicator of poor discipline. He would discuss this with LTC Milner later.

The briefs with Team Anvil and Team Cobra went much smoother. The commanders were waiting with a detailed sketch of their BPs; established RFLs, should Team Dagger conduct passage of lines; and marked and coordinated bypass routes through the EAs. CPT Hernandez and CPT Wang seemed to have the answers to the questions posed by the Team Dagger leaders. The process seemed to go much smoother at each of these positions.

Team Dagger drove through the entire task force engagement area coordinating with each of the other teams. CPT Crafton identified a location on the farthest edge of the EA that would be ideal to establish a hasty defense following a successful counterattack passing through any of the teams. By identifying this single point for consolidation, reorganization, and establishment of hasty defensive positions, CPT Crafton made it simple for his leaders, regardless of how they may be committed. Team Dagger stopped and identified how each of the platoons would occupy hasty defensive positions there and discussed consolidation and reorganization procedures, an impromptu rehearsal. CPT Crafton also established on-call fire control measures, including direct and indirect fire, for the planned location of the potential hasty defense. The fire support officer (FSO) recorded them and made a note to ensure they were sent to the task force TOC for inclusion in the graphic control measures, so all the teams had access to them.

CPT Crafton realized the importance of understanding the scout platoon's screen mission for the task force, but did not want to compromise its positions by driving forward with his large recon element. He had arranged a meeting with 1LT Hendrickson, the scout platoon leader at Team Anvil's BP. 1LT Hendrickson was right on time. Team Dagger's leaders gathered as 1LT Hendrickson briefed each of the scout locations, the platoon mission, decision points as depicted on the decision support matrix, and targets they had refined from the task force order. This was tremendously useful not only for identifying the scout locations but for understanding how the scout platoon's mission supported the defense in the main battle area. CPT Crafton verified the locations on the BFT against the analog map. He saw that the task force FSO had already established no-fire areas on the scout locations. All of the scout teams had plans to collapse the screen and conduct a rearward passage of lines (RPOL), with the exception of one team that would remain in place on the western flank to continue to provide observation throughout the defense. CPT Crafton and the other leaders made particular note of that observation. He established a plan within Team Dagger to track and report on the company net when the screen had collapsed and all teams had conducted RPOL, as they reported on the task force command net. This would ensure they were all aware if any of the scout teams were unable to displace and conduct RPOL and give them awareness of any team that might still be forward of the main defenses.

Along the way, 1LT Farmer identified three positions that overlooked the entire task force main battle area. He approached CPT Crafton. "Sir, I'd like to position the Bradley Fire Support Team vehicle in the primary position in the high ground there," he said, pointing to the highest terrain feature behind the BPs, "where I can place the B-FiST in cover and concealment and dismount and remote to the vehicle, allowing me to be able to observe most of the engagement area, specifically the triggers we identified for the targets covering the obstacles. I'd like to position the forward observer teams from the Bradley platoons there and there," again indicating positions from which engagement area and primary routes could be observed, "so that we would have observation all of the BPs, the engagement area, and Team Dagger's potential maneuver routes. This also allows us to provide redundant coverage of the scout platoon's targets, as Lieutenant Hendrickson just briefed."

CPT Crafton agreed. He had considered the same locations as likely observation posts. He knew his platoon leaders understood that keeping forward observers (FOs) in the fighting vehicles limited their ability to observe and call for fire. "Make it happen." He knew 1LT Farmer would ensure that the task force graphics were updated to include the Ops slides; that restrictive fire areas would be established; and that his FO teams would be briefed on the concept of the operation, triggers, target responsibility, and everything else they needed to know. These would be Team Dagger's eyes to help confirm scout reports and provide updates as the battle progressed in the engagement area. CPT Crafton would rely heavily not only on their ability to provide fires but to provide critical information at critical times that affected Team Dagger's mission.

> **POINT: Position observers where they are able to observe established triggers and targets to execute the fires plan. Consider redundant observation with primary and alternate observers for targets and triggers.**

After a grueling six hours, CPT Crafton felt that he and his leaders gained a significant understanding of the task force defense and their roles. He was concerned, however, with Team Badger's shift of its battle position. Now it did not look as though the team BPs were effectively tied, as described by the task force commander. It was another issue he would have to address with MAJ Santiago or LTC Milner. For now, he needed to get his leaders back to the Soldiers and continue preparation.

Team Dagger
Tactical Assembly Area
H-36 Hours (1800L)

Preparations in the assembly area continued, and platoon leaders and noncommissioned officers (NCOs) had a chance to check on progress made while they were on reconnaissance. A couple of issues with the tanks needed to be addressed. Fortunately, CPT Crafton could see that the mechanics who had been attached to the task force from the brigade support battalion were working on them. It was best to identify those issues now rather than later, with little time to react before enemy contact. This was a good sign that his NCOs had left the Soldiers with clear guidance and that the Soldiers were making things happen in the leaders' absence.

Once again the leaders from Team Dagger gathered at the terrain model. CPT Crafton smiled as he saw that SGT Masters and SPC Waring had already updated the terrain model with Team Badger's refined battle position, target reference points, restrictive fire lines, and other key information. No doubt 1LT Loggins had updated them and ensured the terrain model reflected what they had learned on the recon.

The rehearsal had gone more smoothly than CPT Crafton expected. Clearly the recon, and the chance for Team Dagger to see firsthand the battle positions and engagement area, had paid dividends. During the rehearsal, each platoon leader walked the terrain model to simulate his platoon's actions while the other leaders observed.

1LT Farmer simulated the planned scheme of fires, at times indicating that a primary observer was unable to execute planned fires, requiring an alternate observer to make the call during the rehearsal. Alternate observers included platoon leaders who were not necessarily trained artillery observers but had the responsibility to call for planned fires. The fire support officer reiterated that the primary frequency for fires within Team Dagger would be on its command net. The Bradley Fire Support Team vehicle (FiST) would relay calls for fire to the task force fire support element (FSE) on the task force fires net.

SGT Moreno, the communications NCO, followed 1LT Farmer: "Sir, I have already been around to all of your vehicles to make sure your Soldiers had the radios ready to go. The task force fires net is loaded in channel six on all of your radios in case the FiST is off the net for any reason and you need to reach the task force FSE directly. Channel one is the company command net; channel two is your platoon net; the task force command net is loaded on channel three; the task force O/I net is on channel four; and the task force A/L net is on five. You should primarily only need channels one and two on your two radios, but the others are pre-loaded, just in case."

Again, CPT Crafton's confidence was boosted as he heard that SGT Moreno had taken the initiative to ensure the important frequencies were loaded in all the radios. This came from a lesson learned the hard way at the National Training Center when, at a critical moment in the force-on-force battle, his FiST had been a "MILES kill" and was unable to call for fires. It seemed like an eternity before CPT Crafton could load the task force fires net, and even then he was the only one in Team Dagger able to get that accomplished. Ever since, each vehicle's driver had been pretty good about loading the important frequencies, and SGT Moreno had personally verified them. CPT Crafton concluded the rehearsal by updating the timeline. "OK, we are just a couple of hours away from our night recon. Get back and check on things and make sure your Soldiers get an update on what we have learned so far. We will be ready to go at 2100. I want it to be dark, but I don't want to spend all night. Tomorrow the task force fire support rehearsal is at 1100, and the task force combined arms rehearsal is at 1400. I want leaders, to the maximum extent possible, to listen in on those rehearsals, platoon leaders at a minimum, but maximize participation. Scouts are out tomorrow evening, and we need to be ready to go by then. I am expecting an update from the S-2, and I will brief you when I hear anything new."

> **POINT:** Rehearsals are key to synchronization. They provide visibility on gaps in the plan and allow leaders to account for these gaps. Include everyone in rehearsals. Everyone must know the plan and individual responsibilities. This improves Soldier, leader, and team performance.

About that time, SGT Masters came hurrying. "Sir, Mustang Six just called and wants the commanders at the TOC in 30 minutes."

"Got it, thanks," CPT Crafton replied. "Any questions?" he asked the leaders.

After addressing some minor issues that his platoons were having in preparation, he turned to 1LT Loggins. "XO, I want you to come with me. You need to be up to speed. When we get back, we'll both update the platoon leaders and platoon sergeants. Lieutenant Warrington, be ready to lead the night recon. I doubt we'll be back in time." CPT Crafton knew he could rely on 1LT Warrington. As much as he wanted to be there for the recon, he knew his leaders had to operate under the philosophy of mission command, even for rehearsals and recons, not just in combat. He understood the importance of mutual trust and shared understanding and had provided a clear intent to guide his subordinates' actions while promoting freedom of action and initiative.

Task Force Mustang
Tactical Operations Center
H-34 Hours (2000L)

LTC Milner was having discussions with MAJ Santiago and CPT Robinson in the tactical operations center when CPT Crafton entered. He could sense that LTC Milner was concerned. The other commanders arrived, and LTC Milner began the update.

"We just got word from Mayor Dovzhenko. He says that several men arrived in Voloslav over the last 24 hours. There were six calls on the brigade report hotline with similar reports. Some reports indicate identification of weapons with at least some of the men. Brigade believes they could be irregular forces sent ahead of the main attack. Their intent really is unknown right now. Brigade is working with the task force remaining in Voloslav, but we need to be aware that they could potentially attack Voloslav through various means and are also capable of launching isolated attacks on our defensive positions from Voloslav. The S-2 is talking to brigade for updates, and I will let you know if anything new develops."

CPT Robinson continued with the update on the enemy situation. "It appears as though the enemy brigade may have more of the new electronic warfare jamming systems than we originally thought." He showed the commanders several printed photos. "Here are some images captured from the last 24 hours, taken by the unmanned aerial vehicle. We believe we have identified four separate systems. We're unsure if they are using decoys or if they are functional. We should anticipate the worst. We also observed vehicle preparations continuing, and we now expect that they will begin tactical movement within 16 hours. We anticipate, based on tactical rate of movement, they should arrive in the engagement area, along the most likely avenue of approach, no later than first light, around 0600 the day after tomorrow."

> **POINT: Intelligence preparation of the battlefield (IPB) is a continuous process. It is used to systematically analyze the mission variables in an area of interest to determine their effect on operations. Enemy situations are fluid. Leaders need to develop and maintain a high degree of situational understanding.**

MAJ Santiago followed: "Updated graphics are posted on Blue Force Tracker. You should all be able to see now. In particular, note Team Dagger's Bradley Fire Support Team vehicle and forward observers with established no-fire areas. Also note we have adjusted the restrictive fire lines between the teams to reflect Team Badger's updated position. The brigade civil affairs operations officer, S-9, has coordinated for a civil affairs team to assist in potential evacuation of noncombatants, including interpreters. They have established a collection point, seen on the graphics. Teams should direct any civilians or refugees to the collection point. The brigade team has a plan to evacuate along the designated route to Voloslav. We have tried to minimize the impact on company/teams in dealing with that possibility."

LTC Milner grumbled under his breath. He was not upset that Team Badger had adjusted its battle position so drastically as much as he was irritated that the Team Anvil and Team Cobra commanders had been the ones to report the location change and update the restrictive fire lines. He had not heard anything from Team Badger. How could it not report something so critical, ASAP? At the same time, he was relieved that brigade seemed to have a plan to support the task force, should civilians be encountered in the engagement area or the battle positions. The team was located right where CPT Crafton had recommended initially, then confirmed feasibility during his recon.

> **POINT: Ensure graphics are current and distributed to subordinate elements. Maintenance of real-time mission command information system graphics is critical for a common operational picture. Analog systems should reflect the same information and graphics.**

The rest of the staff gave brief updates to include specific due-outs to the company teams. All in all, preparations across the task force seemed to go well, with very few issues.

At the conclusion of the brief, CPT Crafton again met with LTC Milner. "Sir, I'm a little concerned that there is now a potential gap that the enemy may exploit, particularly between Team Badger and Team Anvil."

LTC Milner had the same thought. "I've addressed that with the commanders. They are all adjusting positions to account for the gap." LTC Milner was annoyed that at this point in BP preparations, they were adjusting for something that should have been identified much sooner. "I still need your team to pay attention to that area. It still concerns me as a vulnerability."

"Yes, sir. I also got with the signal officer and I think we are straight now on signals. I'll send a vehicle runner to the TOC to indicate commitment, should we lose communication. As an emergency and immediate means, I will deploy a red star cluster upon committing to the counterattack. We identified specific landmarks in the engagement area during our recon to each of the BPs, and we have excellent observation from our established observation posts. I know your criteria for potentially supporting another company team is reduction to 60 percent combat power, but I think that may be difficult to determine."

"You're right," LTC Milner replied. "That sort of situation will require a judgment call. I used 60 percent as the criteria, but keep in mind the intent and end state: to deny penetration of the defensive position and entry to Voloslav. That's more important than numbers when making the decision. Again, this is my decision, but you need to be ready to execute within the intent."

"Yes, sir." CPT Crafton understood. He was glad he had a leader like LTC Milner. It helped. But he still felt uneasy about potentially needing to act without his direction. There were a lot of factors to consider.

Seeing the concern on the captain's face, LTC Milner encouraged him. "CPT Crafton, I have the utmost confidence in your leadership. Don't question your judgment. When it comes time, you will know what to do. Don't second-guess yourself."

CPT Crafton felt better, but it was still a huge responsibility. Consideration of all the options helped him feel more comfortable with weighing the potential decisions. There was one more thing that he had been thinking about.

"Sir, I've got Sergeant Masters and Specialist Waring working out of my command vehicle. They have been monitoring Blue Force Tracker and the task force command net for me, ensuring that our information is updated and current. They have been great, but it's a lot to handle considering their training background. If I could get an analyst from the S-2 shop, it would definitely help me supplement this team, kind of a company intelligence support team concept as outlined in the Center for Army Lessons Learned CoIST Handbook. I know that would sting for the S-2, but it would really help us track the battle from unmanned aerial system feeds to first contact with the scouts to the enemy's reaching the engagement area. I think it's important to have the clearest possible understanding of the potential commitment of the reserve. What do you think?"

LTC Milner thought about that for a moment. He was not surprised that CPT Crafton had used talent management to form an adaptive and cohesive team. Leveraging his available personnel in this manner was supported by the very principles of improving Soldier, leader, and team performance and developing capable formations. CPT Robinson definitely had his hands full. He certainly could not afford to divvy up his staff for all the teams to have a CoIST. It certainly was unconventional. But the more he thought about it, the more it made sense. The reserve, if committed, would most likely be the decisive operation. He was asking a lot from CPT Crafton. He would agree to it.

"Captain Robinson, come here." LTC Milner explained the idea. "I want you to send an analyst with Captain Crafton to supplement his command post leading up to the battle. I know it will be painful for the S-2 shop, but you need to send somebody that is capable of really providing quality analysis. He will be with Team Dagger for the duration of the battle."

> **POINT: Agile and adaptive leaders apply creative and innovative solutions to complex problems. Tactics, techniques, and procedures; best practices; and doctrine are developed through application of creative solutions. Leaders must be aware of Soldiers' unique skills and abilities, managing talent to develop a more capable formation.**

CPT Crafton could sense that CPT Robinson wasn't tickled with the idea. He caught his glare as LTC Milner was explaining. But he knew CPT Robinson realized that this made sense. He also knew CPT Robinson would send him his very best. He was a team player.

CPT Robinson got SPC Flynn and instructed him to get his things together. CPT Crafton had interacted frequently with SPC Flynn, usually when CPT Robinson was out of the TOC for whatever reason. The specialist was sharp; he would be just the guy. While SPC Flynn gathered his essential gear and equipment, CPT Crafton made sure to get with each of the primary staff members prior to leaving the TOC, just to make sure nothing had changed. He was pleased that the task force staff seemed to be up to date on reports from Team Dagger. Things seemed to be in order, with everybody on the same page.

SPC Flynn loaded his equipment and they departed back to the assembly area. CPT Crafton was anxious to hear how the recon went.

Team Dagger
Tactical Assembly Area
H-30 Hours (2400L)

CPT Crafton was starting to feel worn. During the past two days he seemed to go nonstop. He needed some rest, but there were a couple of things he had to get done first.

He linked up SPC Flynn with SGT Masters and SPC Waring. The commander gave them a quick rundown of his vision of the company intelligence support team (CoIST) and what they needed to do. They would operate from the command vehicle and monitor the task force O/I net. They would provide updates over the team command net, keeping CPT Crafton and the other leaders informed as the battle progressed.

SPC Flynn retrieved one of his bags and pulled some intelligence products that CPT Robinson had sent with him. They included the templated enemy order of battle, most likely and most dangerous courses of action, avenues of approach, and other key battle-tracking information. SPC Flynn gave SGT Masters and SPC Waring a quick overview of the products and how they could be used to track the battle. He also pointed out the task force commander's key decisions as they corresponded to enemy actions. CPT Crafton was pleased. The S-2 had clearly sent the right man, and he was clearly prepared.

CPT Crafton left the three as they discussed organization of their CoIST vehicle. He needed to get with 1LT Warrington and find out how the recon had gone. They had arrived back in the assembly area shortly after he had returned from the tactical operations center. He also wanted to see how his Soldiers were faring.

"Lieutenant Warrington," CPT Crafton shouted as his platoon leader hurried from Bradley to Bradley, also checking on his Soldiers. "How did the recon go?"

"Sir, it went well, but we had a couple of hiccups. We had no problem with the routes. Everybody seemed pretty comfortable, even in the dark, after the recon earlier. It was a little slower movement, but we could still identify the key locations we discussed earlier and everybody seemed to really understand. Team Anvil and Team Cobra had easily identifiable markers on the target reference points we saw earlier, but Team Badger hadn't placed markers. We helped them build some thermal markers with ammo cans, diesel, and oil. We mixed the oil and diesel with sand in the cans with holes for ventilation. When ignited they will provide a heat signature for five or six hours or so. We placed infrared and regular chem lights on the friendly side of the cans for visual identification. We all got a chance to look at the

45

TRPs [target reference points] in each of the battle positions through the thermals. I think they're good to go now. But I sure hope Team Badger replaces the fuel and chem lights on its TRPs tomorrow. Here is a copy of the time hacks I had to each of the checkpoints along the routes and the total times of travel. Overall it was roughly one and a half times as long during darkness."

> **POINT: Identification of markers for target reference points should ideally be identifiable through unaided, passive infrared, and thermal observation modes.**

Just as CPT Crafton thought, 1LT Warrington was all over it. The commander would make a point to do a personal recon the next night so he could see the TRPs at night like the rest of his leaders. Then he would know if the thermal, infrared, and visual TRP markers had been replenished. He would also validate the time hacks and overall travel times the platoon leader had provided. It sounded as if 1LT Warrington had done exactly what CPT Crafton would have done had he been there himself.

CPT Crafton made a quick run to each of his platoons, checking on his Soldiers and getting other leaders' perspectives on the recon. He was pleased that they pretty much all indicated the same things. He distributed fliers with evacuation instructions and a strip map for civilians printed in the native language and English. He had taken the time to create this with the interpreter at the TOC. These aids could give instructions to any noncombatants who may be encountered on the battlefield. CPT Crafton also confirmed to his leaders that the evacuation plan they had discussed during the recon was in place with the team from brigade to assist from the collection point.

Most of his Soldiers were down resting. That was good. He knew they had been working hard. It reminded him that he needed to get some sleep. He would make the rounds again tomorrow. It was important for him to see his Soldiers and for them to see him. He needed the perspective of the enlisted Soldiers, not just his NCO and officer leaders.

Just then, 1SG Young tracked him down. "Sir, you've got two minutes to get in your sack! Then I'm going to tackle you and put you there myself! Don't run yourself into the ground!"

CPT Crafton knew Top was right. He was probably serious about tackling, too. "Sir, we saved you a meal. It's probably not hot now, but it's waiting for you." CPT Crafton smiled, knowing that 1SG Young had taken care of the Soldiers in his same grumpy manner. He got it. He cared. He just had the crusty attitude on the surface. The commander went off to the waiting meal and some sleep.

Team Dagger
Tactical Assembly Area
H-12 Hours (1800L)

CPT Crafton felt the tension mount throughout the Team Dagger assembly area as the time of the anticipated enemy attack drew near. Soldiers hurried to complete preventive maintenance and precombat checks and inspections. The medics had just trooped the line again, and Top had arranged a service with the chaplain earlier in the day. Mail had been delivered, and that had been a big morale boost for the Soldiers.

> **POINT: Precombat checks and inspections, (PCCs/PCIs) including maintenance, fuel, ammunition, supply, and other activities, are ongoing processes. Leaders must ensure PCCs/PCIs are conducted to standard to ensure continued readiness.**

Now the leaders gathered once again for a rehearsal before moving to the alternate assembly area. The platoon leaders walked the terrain model, simulating actions for each contingency. The rehearsal was smoother, quicker now. For Team Dagger, actions had become familiar and instinctual. CPT Crafton was pleased. He was satisfied that his leaders understood the intent, the plan, and the desired end state. He was confident that his insistence on rehearsing again and again would pay off in the heat of battle.

As the rehearsal concluded, the commander insisted that his leaders eat, hydrate, and get some rest. It was going to be a long, difficult 24 hours ahead for Team Dagger. 1SG Young had the thermal panel out, and it would be only a few minutes until the crews completed bore sighting, probably for the last time before battle.

CPT Crafton knew he needed rest, too. But he needed to visit the battle positions one more time to see if anything had changed significantly and to see the marked target reference points for himself.

Team Dagger
Engagement Area Blackjack
H+45 Minutes (0645L)

It had been a long night. The anticipation of the coming battle heightened tremendously as the initial scout reports came over the net, confirming the enemy's advance along what the S-2 determined was the most likely avenue of approach. It became apparent that the enemy would focus its attack in the vicinity of Battle Position (BP) Badger. Team Dagger had moved to its alternate assembly area in the cover of darkness, better positioning for a potential counterattack and vacating the position that might have been observed by enemy reconnaissance assets.

The company intelligence support team (CoIST) had updated CPT Crafton with initial reports from the scouts and the unmanned aerial system feed over the operations and intelligence net, and through initial contact in the engagement area. The CoIST had collected and analyzed information in the spot reports. Then the radio nets went silent. Nobody called. Nobody responded to calls. CPT Crafton's tension spiked. It was as if he were alone on an island. Yet, he reminded himself, he had gone over this again and again. He knew what to do. He remembered LTC Milner's words of encouragement.

At this point he had a pretty good idea that Team Dagger would be committed near BP Badger. He decided to send out the route clearance team now. He did not want to slow his potential counterattack force behind the route clearance team.

He could hear the fight raging from the battle positions. It was clear that the enemy was fighting through the obstacles. He huddled with SPC Flynn, SGT Masters, and SPC Waring. SPC Flynn again went over the enemy order of battle as confirmed by the scouts. The last report was that the enemy was deploying into combat formations. It led with motorized forces, seemingly to protect its mechanized assets during initial contact. SPC Flynn predicted they were trailing initial units by about 30 minutes.

CPT Crafton grabbed his binoculars and scanned his observation posts (OPs). He could not talk to his observers at this point, but he had established a signal with them. They would display a VS-17 panel if the mechanized forces were passing the obstacles in any of the company/team engagement areas. Nothing.

Suddenly, the radios came back alive. He heard CPT Hernandez frantically reporting over the task force command net: "Mustang Six, this is Cobra Six. Enemy vehicles are squeezing through between us and Badger. We're holding strong, but we can't effectively engage where they are at, over."

"Badger Six, this is Mustang Six, SITREP, over."

Nothing.

"Dagger Six, this is …"

Commo gone … again. CPT Crafton was frantic. What was he going to say? It sounded like Cobra was still combat effective. CPT Hernandez had not indicated significant losses. He remembered his commander's intent: not to allow penetration and advance to Voloslav. He and SPC Flynn glanced at the refined decision support matrix (DSM) that they had helped MAJ Santiago develop for this contingency. He knew what to do.

He ran to 1LT Warrington. "Get your platoon on the left flank of Team Cobra right now! Vehicles are exploiting the space between them and Team Badger. Remember where we discussed potentially filling the gap, right where ..."

"Sir, I got it. I know just what you're saying. Moving!" 1LT Warrington's platoon moved out.

Though CPT Crafton was anxious as he committed a portion of the task force reserve, this is just what he had discussed with the commander and the staff. He knew it was the right thing to do, right now.

Glancing again through his binos, he now saw as plain as day the VS-17 panel indicating that mechanized vehicles were passing through initial obstacles. Fourth Platoon had already moved out, but it was time now. Again, he glanced at the DSM, but he already knew the information that was before him met the criteria for the decisive point on the matrix.

CPT Crafton frantically tried to reach the tactical operations center (TOC) or the commander on the radio. After a few attempts he fired the star cluster. Team Dagger knew what that meant. Almost immediately the team maneuvered, as rehearsed, toward the engagement area at BP Badger. The vehicle runner, on cue, stopped to get specific instructions from CPT Crafton and went off toward the TOC. CPT Crafton hurriedly sent the draft message on Blue Force Tracker to the commander and TOC, indicating that Team Dagger had begun its counterattack in vicinity of BP Badger. He had drafted several messages ahead of time so he could send them quickly if needed.

> **POINT: Thoroughly understanding the commander's intent and concept of the operation allows leaders to be decisive in conditions of uncertainty and chaos.**

Along the route, Team Dagger encountered a handful of refugees in civilian vehicles still desperately trying to leave the battle zone. Soldiers distributed the fliers that included instructions and a strip map, which brought some relief to the panicked civilians.

1LT Farmer executed the planned fires, including artillery smoke to screen Team Dagger's movement. The preplanned close air support (CAS) was devastating the enemy formations. Meanwhile, the platoons' maneuver to contact seemed perfectly synchronized. CPT Crafton directed the attack helicopters to specific targets as the team maneuvered.

As they closed on the engagement area, his tanks and fighting vehicles were able pass through Team Badger, despite heavy losses it sustained. It was apparent that previous coordination enabled Team Dagger to move seamlessly and maintain momentum, even as it engaged the enemy. CPT Crafton ensured he got confirmation from Team Badger that the restrictive fire line they had coordinated was activated.

POINT: When implementing or activating fire-control measures, confirm that applicable units, direct-fire systems, and indirect fire assets are aware of the fire-control measure. Fire-control measures are ineffective if they are not followed.

Team Dagger methodically tore through the enemy formation. The lethality of the combined fires from the maneuver platoons, artillery, attack aviation, and CAS came together in a symphony of destruction. Once they passed through Team Badger, each of the platoons, aware of its responsibilities in relation to the established target reference points (TRPs), maneuvered in conjunction with the others. The coordinated direct fires were devastating to the enemy because of the efficiency and ability of the platoons to identify and engage targets in their assigned sectors.

Inside the tanks, crews executed battle drills and commands with precision.

"Gunner, HEAT, PC, 1,500 meters, TRP 3!"

"Identified!"

"Up!"

"Fire!"

"On the way!"

"Cease fire."

The Bradley crews operated with the same precision.

"Gunner, missile, two tanks, one o'clock!"

"Identified!"

"Back blast area clear! Fire!"

"On the way!"

"Cease tracking!"

"Moving tank!"

"Identified!"

"Back blast area clear! Fire!"

"On the way!"

"Cease tracking, out of action!"

The established TRPs had served to coordinate target responsibility among the platoons, and for tank and crew commanders to identify targets to the gunners. The recons and rehearsals, during which Team Dagger went over and over the direct-fire plans, paid tremendous dividends.

POINT: References for direct-fire control enable crews to identify targets and coordinate responsibility for targets in an engagement area.

The radios came alive with chatter again as Team Dagger destroyed the last remaining enemy electronic warfare system in the counterattack. In the distance CPT Crafton saw the plume of white phosphorus, planned to orient the CAS aircraft and identify targets. He knew 1LT Farmer was relaying target information to the aircraft through the task force fire support element as Team Dagger advanced. Artillery fires rained on planned targets in the engagement area, providing suppression of advancing fighting vehicles as Team Dagger's direct fires decimated the now-canalized enemy formations. Attack aviation engaged vehicles in the rear of the enemy's formation as the tanks and Bradleys pounded the lead vehicles.

It seemed it was over as quickly as it began. Team Dagger consolidated and reorganized, just as it had rehearsed. CPT Crafton determined that he had lost two Bradleys and had one tank that was immobile due to a damaged track. Although he was devastated at the loss of his 3rd Platoon Leader, 1LT Gaden, and four of his other Soldiers, he knew the losses had been minimized by the team's meticulous planning and preparation. Medics evacuated the three severely wounded Soldiers, but it looked like they were going to make it, thanks to Top's carefully coordinated MEDEVAC plan. They probably were already at the ambulance exchange point and would receive life-saving treatment at an appropriate medical facility within the hour.

CPT Crafton allowed himself to briefly reflect. Every officer, noncommissioned officer, and enlisted Soldier had performed phenomenally. There were no wasted actions. Everybody knew what to do, and Team Dagger made it happen. CPT Crafton was thankful for the outcome and proud of his team's accomplishment of the mission.

"Mustang Six, this is Dagger Six, SITREP follows, break ..." CPT Crafton updated the commander on Team Dagger's combat strength, location, disposition, and ammunition status. He heard the other teams' reports, as well. Task Force Mustang had accomplished the mission and met the commander's intent. But CPT Crafton's heart sank as he heard the outcome for Team Badger. He knew it was not good when he had passed through the battle position. His thoughts turned to CPT Morris and his Soldiers. It would be a difficult road ahead for them.

Engagement Area Blackjack
H+90 Minutes (0730L)

The commander of the enemy brigade was scrambling to recover control of his dwindling forces. After initial dominating success, his unit was now being shredded by the American tanks and Bradley fighting vehicles. How did things turn so quickly?

The attack began just as planned. Of course, the geo-located images the Americans had so foolishly posted on social media sites had helped tremendously in identifying key targets. The enemy commander's own cyber assets had detected increased activity in the area of the American defense. They quickly were able to identify specific users, and better yet, the network of users back in their home country. Posts and information from friends and spouses in America had helped confirm and develop the intelligence his brigade had collected.

The partnerships with local criminal organizations in Voloslav had paid off tremendously. Although there were some differences in their ideals, the partnerships had served all involved parties in their common goal of evicting the Americans from Bolcavia, isolating and defeating Bolcavian Army units, and eventually returning control of Bolcavia to Arcania. And the enemy had been able to coordinate for improvised explosive device attacks against the Americans before the brigade attacked. It had been so easy since the Americans foolishly left their prepared battle position without security. The enemy commander imagined that the Americans were forced to react and turn their attention away from their main battle area.

He had purposefully displaced civilians from the town of Kapustivka. He had been able to integrate a handful of intelligence collectors, posing as civilians, among the population and directed them along the route toward the American defense. This served him well by gaining the ability to provide further confirmation and clarity on his intelligence and by causing the Americans to react to civilians on the battlefield. The confusion and disruption this caused was evident from the reports he received and gained him precious time and space in the midst of the confusion.

He used the social media information, along with the images gathered by the quadcopter operated by a local sympathizer on his payroll, in his planning and targeting processes. Clearly his initial artillery preparatory fires and damage inflicted by the supporting Arcanian attack helicopters had taken a significant toll on the defending American forces. They clearly were unable to react to his approaching formations, and he breached the American obstacles with very little resistance.

He had perfectly calculated the timing to activate his jamming systems, and he could tell, as his formations advanced to initial contact, that the American reaction was clearly impeded by an inability to effectively communicate on their radio nets. But as this new force counterattacked the brigade, one of the first vehicles lost was the last of his new jamming equipment the Arcanian government had supplied just weeks before. His newly trained crew was lost, as well. And now the Americans clearly did not have a problem communicating. Why had they not focused on the tanks and fighting vehicles? How did they know to target the jamming systems? It was probably just dumb luck for the Americans.

Up until contact with the American counterattack force, it seemed as if the enemy brigade would blow through the defenses and be in downtown Voloslav, with initial control of the city, by sundown. Now the commander was hoping he could salvage the remainder of his tattered unit to reorganize and fight another day. But the way things were looking now, all may be lost.

The American artillery, attack helicopters, and close air support, supporting the devastating direct fires from the Abrams tanks and Bradley fighting vehicles, which the Americans so boastfully called the best in the world, were all now pounding his unit into oblivion. Perhaps these machines really were as good as the Americans claimed. Or perhaps their Soldiers and Airmen were really that good. Or maybe he had just run into General Patton himself. It didn't matter at this point. The inevitable end seemed near as he listened to the reports of his subordinate commanders, the ones who were still alive, indicate that their combat power and personnel were all but lost.

Just then, a Hellfire missile tore through the turret of the enemy commander's vehicle, and his worried thoughts no longer mattered as he died an explosive death.

Task Force Mustang
Tactical Operations Center
H+3 Hours (0900L)

LTC Milner slumped in near exhaustion in his chair in the tactical operations center. The adrenaline of battle had left him, and the resulting crash was hitting him hard. He could see the same results in his staff members as they gathered reports from the teams and orchestrated recovery assets, MEDEVAC, and other necessary post-battle actions.

The battle had seemed to be here and over in a flash even though the frustration of failing communications seemed to last an eternity. Through intermittent communications, LTC Milner fought to track the situation from each team on combat power, enemy actions, friendly actions, and ammo status. It took diligence on the part of the staff to piece together the information through voice communications or Blue Force Tracker. The commanders had done a good job in trying to report regularly, but the interruption of communications had caused the staff and LTC Milner to make assumptions at times.

His task force held up nicely, though Team Badger was in pretty bad shape. LTC Milner shook his head. CPT Morris was not a bad officer; he just didn't pay attention to detail the way the other commanders did. He knew CPT Morris would be taking the loss of most of his company hard.

Fortunately, CPT Crafton and Team Dagger had executed nearly flawlessly within his intent. If asked to describe an agile, adaptive, and innovative leader who thrives in conditions of uncertainty and chaos, LTC Milner would definitely refer to CPT Crafton. LTC Milner had always driven himself to be better able to visualize, describe, direct, lead, and assess in a complex environments. He saw a reflection of that in CPT Crafton.

Becoming the decisive operation, CPT Crafton's team had decimated the enemy during the counterattack. LTC Milner nodded his head as he thought, "Yes, I picked the right team for that mission."

References

Army Doctrine Publication (ADP) 3-0, *Unified Land Operations,* October 2011

ADP 3-07, *Stability*, August 2012

ADP 3-09, *Fires*, August 2012

ADP 3-90, *Offense and Defense,* August 2012

Army Doctrine Reference Publication (ADRP) 1-03, *The Army Universal Task List,* October 2015

ADRP 3-0, *Unified Land Operations,* May 2012

ADRP 3-07, *Stability*, August 2012

ADRP 3-09, *Fires*, August 2012

ADRP 3-90, *Offense and Defense*, August 2012

Army Techniques Publication 3-20.15, *Tank Platoon*, December 2012

Army Tactics, Techniques, and Procedures 3-21.71, *Mechanized Infantry Platoon and Squad (Bradley),* November 2010

Field Manual (FM) 3-09, *Field Artillery Operations and Fire Support*, April 2014

FM 3-90-1, *Offense and Defense Volume 1*, March 2013

FM 6-0, *Commander and Staff Organization and Operations*, May 2014

Training Circular (TC) 7-100, *Hybrid Threat*, November 2010

TC 7-100.2, *Opposing Force Tactics*, December 2011

TC 7-100.3, *Irregular Opposing Forces*, January 2014

TC 7-100.4, *Hybrid Thread Force Structure Organization Guide*, June 2015

PROVIDE US YOUR INPUT

To help you access information quickly and efficiently, the Center for Army Lessons Learned (CALL) posts all publications, along with numerous other useful products, on the CALL website.

PROVIDE FEEDBACK OR REQUEST INFORMATION

http://call.army.mil

If you have any comments, suggestions, or requests for information (RFIs), use the "Contact Us" link on the CALL home page.

PROVIDE LESSONS AND BEST PRACTICES OR SUBMIT AN AFTER ACTION REVIEW (AAR)

If your unit has identified lessons or best practices or would like to submit an AAR, please contact CALL using the following information:

Telephone: DSN 552-9569/9533; Commercial 913-684-9569/9533

Fax: DSN 552-4387; Commercial 913-684-4387

Mailing Address: **Center for Army Lessons Learned**
                               ATTN: Chief, Collection Division
                               10 Meade Ave., Bldg. 50
                               Fort Leavenworth, KS 66027-1350

TO REQUEST COPIES OF THIS PUBLICATION

If you would like copies of this publication, please submit your request on the CALL restricted site at <https://call2.army.mil> (CAC login required). Click on "Request for Publications." Please fill in all the information, including your unit name and street address. Please include building number and street for military posts.

NOTE: Some CALL publications are no longer available in print. Digital publications are available clicking on "Publications by Type" under "Resources" tab on the CALL restricted website.

PRODUCTS AVAILABLE ONLINE

CENTER FOR ARMY LESSONS LEARNED

Access and download information from CALL's website. CALL also offers Web-based access to the CALL archives. The CALL restricted website address is:

http://call.army.mil

CALL produces the following publications on a variety of subjects:

- **Handbooks**
- **Bulletins, Newsletters, and Trends Reports**
- **Special Studies**
- *News From the Front*
- **Training Lessons and Best Practices**
- **Initial Impressions Reports**

COMBINED ARMS CENTER (CAC)
Additional Publications and Resources

The CAC home page address is:

http://usacac.army.mil

Center for Army Leadership (CAL)

CAL plans and programs leadership instruction, doctrine, and research. CAL integrates and synchronizes the Professional Military Education Systems and Civilian Education System. Find CAL products at <http://usacac.army.mil/cac2/cal>.

Combat Studies Institute (CSI)

CSI is a military history think tank that produces timely and relevant military history and contemporary operational history. Find CSI products at <http://usacac.army.mil/cac2/csi/csipubs.asp>.

Combined Arms Doctrine Directorate (CADD)

CADD develops, writes, and updates Army doctrine at the corps and division level. Find the doctrinal publications at either the Army Publishing Directorate (APD) <http://www.apd.army.mil> or the Central Army Registry (formerly known as the Reimer Digital Library) <http://www.adtdl.army.mil>.

Foreign Military Studies Office (FMSO)

FMSO is a research and analysis center on Fort Leavenworth under the TRADOC G2. FMSO manages and conducts analytical programs focused on emerging and asymmetric threats, regional military and security developments, and other issues that define evolving operational environments around the world. Find FMSO products at <http://fmso.leavenworth.army.mil>.

Military Review (MR)

MR is a revered journal that provides a forum for original thought and debate on the art and science of land warfare and other issues of current interest to the U.S. Army and the Department of Defense. Find MR at <http://usacac.army.mil/cac2/militaryreview>.

TRADOC Intelligence Support Activity (TRISA)

TRISA is a field agency of the TRADOC G2 and a tenant organization on Fort Leavenworth. TRISA is responsible for the development of intelligence products to support the policy-making, training, combat development, models, and simulations arenas. Find TRISA at <https://atn.army.mil/media/dat/TRISA/trisa.aspx> (CAC login required).

Capability Development Integration Directorate (CDID)

CDID conducts analysis, experimentation, and integration to identify future requirements and manage current capabilities that enable the Army, as part of the Joint Force, to exercise Mission Command and to operationalize the Human Dimension. Find CDID at <http://usacac.army.mil/organizations/mccoe/cdid>.

Joint Center for International Security Force Assistance (JCISFA)

JCISFA's mission is to capture and analyze security force assistance (SFA) lessons from contemporary operations to advise combatant commands and military departments on appropriate doctrine; practices; and proven tactics, techniques, and procedures (TTP) to prepare for and conduct SFA missions efficiently. JCISFA was created to institutionalize SFA across DOD and serve as the DOD SFA Center of Excellence. Find JCISFA at <https://jcisfa.jcs.mil/Public/Index.aspx>.

Support CAC in the exchange of information by telling us about your successes so they may be shared and become Army successes.

Made in the USA
Columbia, SC
14 January 2020